# WINGS OVER WASHINGTON

# WINGS OVER WASHINGTON

MINERS LANDING PRESS

Copyright © 2016 Miners Landing Press

All rights reserved.

No part of this book may be reproduced, transmitted, or stored in an information retrieval system in any form or by any means, graphic, electronic, or mechanical, including photocopying, taping, and recording, without prior permission in writing from the publisher.

Library of Congress Cataloging-in-Publication Data is available.

ISBN: 978-0-9860867-9-3

Printed in China
First edition 2016

Miners Landing Press
1301 Alaskan Way
Seattle, WA 98101
Please visit us at www.MinersLanding.com

Produced by Girl Friday Productions, LLC
www.girlfridayproductions.com

**FRONT COVER:** *The alpenglow at Mount Rainier tints the sky red.*

*We do not inherit the earth from our ancestors;
we borrow it from our children.*

Chief Seattle, 1854

# CONTENTS

| | | |
|---|---|---|
| | INTRODUCTION | 2 |
| CHAPTER 1 | COASTLINE | 4 |
| CHAPTER 2 | OLYMPIC PENINSULA | 18 |
| CHAPTER 3 | PUGET SOUND | 32 |
| CHAPTER 4 | SAN JUAN ISLANDS | 46 |
| CHAPTER 5 | NORTH CASCADES | 60 |
| CHAPTER 6 | THE PALOUSE AND EASTERN WASHINGTON | 74 |
| CHAPTER 7 | WINE COUNTRY | 88 |
| CHAPTER 8 | COLUMBIA RIVER AND THE GORGE | 102 |
| CHAPTER 9 | VOLCANO COUNTRY | 116 |
| CHAPTER 10 | SEATTLE | 130 |
| | THE MAKING OF WINGS OVER WASHINGTON | 146 |
| | ACKNOWLEDGMENTS | 150 |
| | ABOUT MINERS LANDING | 150 |
| | IMAGE CREDITS | 150 |

*Miners Landing today.*

# INTRODUCTION

Welcome to *Wings Over Washington*! We are thrilled to share with you the natural beauty, culture, and history of Washington State. Our family is proud to have had a home on Seattle's waterfront for almost half a century. As Washington's largest city, Seattle provides visitors and locals a wealth of experiences, but our state has much to offer beyond Seattle's city limits. Showcasing these many marvels is the inspiration for the Wings Over Washington attraction, as well as this accompanying book. You'll experience the thrill of the pounding Pacific surf, the exhilaration of a hot-air-balloon ride over wine country, the grandeur of the Columbia River Gorge, and so much more.

On Pier 57, we strive to create new opportunities to explore the flavor of the Pacific Northwest. Our restaurant the Crab Pot was inspired by our family memories of feasting on freshly caught crab in the most northwest of ways: pouring great piles of cooked crab onto a newspaper-covered table and digging in. The Great Wheel at the end of Pier 57 provides a perspective of Western Washington and its largest city like no other, and the Miners Landing building evokes the salty feel of old Seattle.

Like the other attractions at Pier 57, Wings Over Washington was designed to provide a unique view of our beautiful state, and an opportunity to bring you into the Pacific Northwest we know and love. The film provides an eagle-eyed look at the nooks and crannies of the diverse and wondrous Evergreen State, using state-of-the-art filmmaking and design to celebrate the things we love most. How appropriate in this city, which has grown up alongside some of the great advances in aviation and technology. We're excited to be both a reminder of old Seattle and a part of a new, vibrant city.

But we wanted to show you even more of Washington than we could fit into the Wings Over Washington film—the harbor seals and octopuses beyond the coastline, the mossy and silent sanctuary in Olympic National Park known as One Square Inch, Mount Saint Helens before and after the great eruption. That's where this book comes in.

*Wings Over Washington*, the book, lets us give you all the things we can't fit into a film or a ride and provides a way for you to bring the beauty of Washington home—whether you're a Seattle native or from the other side of the globe.

Our family has been on Pier 57 since the 1960s, and we take great pride in sharing its history. As one of the most historically important sites in Seattle—near where the *Portland* arrived with a ton of gold from Alaska, kicking off the gold rush and making Seattle a city—it's the perfect home for this unique experience. We feel like a part of the story of Seattle, too, and having the opportunity to create an attraction that shows off Washington's breathtaking beauty is something special for us.

We hope that *Wings Over Washington* will allow you to relish your memories of our great state—whether you experienced all its wonders firsthand or on Pier 57.

Sincerely,

Kyle Griffith

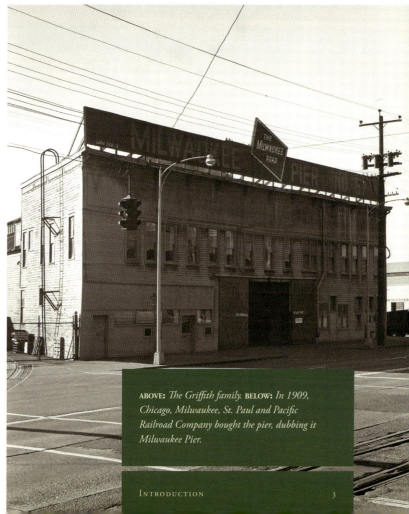

**ABOVE:** *The Griffith family.* **BELOW:** *In 1909, Chicago, Milwaukee, St. Paul and Pacific Railroad Company bought the pier, dubbing it Milwaukee Pier.*

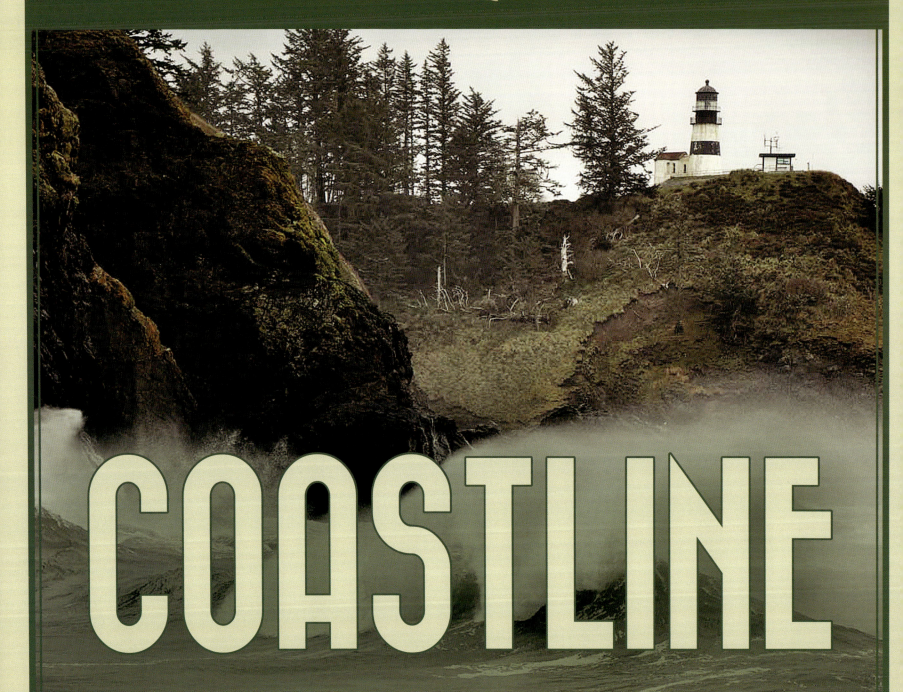

CHAPTER 1

COASTLINE

# PEWTER WAVES POUND THE COAST.

They roll in, streaming white banners of foam, throwing sprays of gulls skyward, and draping the sand with ribbons of seaweed. Dungeness crabs scuttle sideways across the beach. For miles on end there is sand.

Seaward, sea stacks—geological landforms—rise out of the surf. Beyond them, cargo ships and fishing vessels careen through the waters. The woods encroach on the sand, along which lay monstrous driftwood logs between green and yellow beach grasses waving in the wind. Inland, the humus that has collected in the laced roots and branches of fallen trees forms a forest floor that is spongy and trampoline-like. Fir cones fall in relative silence here where you can't even hear the surf, and during autumn the forest turns bright with the orange-yellow of chanterelle mushrooms pushing through the duff.

The Washington coast stretches across an amazing 3,026 miles of shoreline, between where the Columbia River empties into the Pacific Ocean alongside Oregon and the Canada border off the Strait of Georgia. The state's western edge, where land meets the ocean, is the wildest and most remote part of Washington, with mile upon mile of beach.

At the southern end, just across from Oregon, the rocky, moss-covered headland of Cape Disappointment juts like a thumb into the Columbia River and the Pacific Ocean. The point was so named by Captain John Meares, who turned his ship around here in 1788, thereby failing to discover the Columbia River. And it was here that the Lewis and Clark expedition achieved its cross-continent mission in 1805. Today, the name of Cape Disappointment doesn't seem appropriate. The stunning headlands are topped by the West Coast's oldest working lighthouse, surrounded by a large state park, and where the rocks end, seemingly endless beach begins.

**ABOVE:** *The sun ascends over Second Beach at La Push.* **BELOW:** *Sea stacks rise out of the surf at Olympic National Park's Ruby Beach.*

Chapter 1: Coastline

North of here on a little spit of land comes Long Beach. Dune grasses wave alongside the 8.3-mile-long Lewis and Clark Discovery Trail that stretches between Ilwaco and Long Beach, nearly hiding the four monuments that honor the area's history: a nine-foot-tall etched basalt monolith, a bronze sculpture of William Clark with a sturgeon, a 19-foot bronze sculpture demarking the most Northwest point reached by Lewis and Clark, and the skeleton of a gray whale that washed ashore here in 2000. With its 27-mile-long beach—the longest drivable beach in the United States—and boardwalks, the town of Long Beach is aptly named. The spit, averaging 1.5 miles in width, is hemmed in by the Pacific Ocean to the west and Willapa Bay to the east, home to a thriving oyster-farming culture and a bay so prolific it sent oysters in the millions to San Francisco during the California gold rush.

Farther north are tiny Grayland and the deep-sea-fishing hub of Westport. Here, surf music streams out of speakers not far from a rocky jetty where wet-suit-clad surfers congregate, and commercial and recreational fishing vessels chug into the largest marina on the Pacific Northwest's outer coast. Across Grays Harbor is Aberdeen, once home to nearly 40 sawmills and a booming lumber business, and made famous in the 1990s by many a lyric. Aberdeen was the hometown of Kurt Cobain—lead singer, guitarist, and primary songwriter for the band Nirvana.

And still the beach stretches on, beginning again at the northern mouth of Grays Harbor at Ocean Shores, with its shallow canals, and endless sand for watching shorebird migrations and kite flying. It rolls north to the petite town of Moclips at the mouth of the Moclips River and continues on through the Quinault Reservation—where conifer forests meet the ocean along land of the western coast Salish people, the Quinault Indian Nation. The Washington coastline extends to Ruby Beach, notable for its sea stacks, and then to La Push.

**LEFT:** *Birds congregate at low tide at Westport Beach.* **ABOVE:** *During razor-clam season openings, crowds of clammers descend on Long Beach and other nearby beaches.* **BELOW:** *A view of the Pacific from Cape Disappointment.*

CHAPTER 1: COASTLINE     7

THIS PAGE: *A keyhole sea stack at Ruby Beach.*
OPPOSITE: *Sunset at La Push's Second Beach.*

Sea stacks may sound like something out of a sci-fi movie, but in fact the rock formations that jut out of the sea—often topped by sea lions, seagulls, or a solitary tree—are former headlands that have been eroded from the mainland. Although these promontories once formed a cliff, over time that land wore away in the pounding surf. Initially, the waves carved bridges or holes in the rock, but eventually even those crumbled, leaving only the distinct, spectacular sea stacks.

Just southwest of Forks, La Push is the jumping-off point for many coastal backpacking expeditions. From here north, the land turns from sand to long stretches of rock ledges that expose countless tide pools teeming with life.

Beyond the nesting eagles, dripping headlands, and monuments to ships lost on rocky shoals are Lake Ozette—the largest unaltered, natural lake in the state—and Shi Shi Beach, where rain-forest trails lead to beach walks decorated by sea stacks and rocky arches, and tide pools dappled by sea anemones and a rainbow of starfish.

Finally, there is Cape Alava, the westernmost point in the continental United States. Nearby, the coast bends around Cape Flattery with its rugged, tree-topped cliffs where eagles and osprey cavort, and its clear salt water, alive with gray whales and orcas, sea lions and sea otters. The ocean rushes around the cape and into Neah Bay, home of the Makah Tribe, known for its whaling traditions and art production, and becomes part of the mighty Strait of Juan de Fuca.

# OUR EDIBLE COAST

Come spring and late fall, the hearty don waders and headlamps, grab buckets and clam guns and shovels, and flock to the Pacific Ocean coast. Here, along the surf, enormous and delicious razor clams burrow their way inches below the receding tide line.

Razor clams aren't the only edibles found on Washington shores. In saline and brackish waters some of the most delicious oysters grow wild and in farms. The Shigoku oyster was invented here by growing standard Pacific oysters in bags attached to floats that move with the tide, thereby tumbling the oyster. Every time the oyster gets agitated, it flexes its muscles to close its shell, in the end creating a deep cup and exceptionally firm flesh. Sea vegetables flourish in Washington, too. In fact, some chefs have begun harvesting bull kelp—long, ropelike seaweed with a bulbous end—and using the seeds like caper berries. Of course, when it comes to seafood, Washington is best known for its sweet, meaty Dungeness crab and its wild salmon.

The shoreline is also bountiful. Come fall, chanterelle mushrooms abound in the woods along the coast from Ozette to Ilwaco. And hundreds of acres of cranberry farms fill the wetlands in and around the Long Beach Peninsula.

**OPPOSITE:** *Traditional smoked salmon at the Lummi Indian Reservation.* **LEFT:** *Tulalip tribal members check Dungeness crabs for size and sex.* **ABOVE:** *Salmon swim up the Sol Duc River falls to spawn.* **BELOW:** *A Makah tribe salmon catch photographed in 1958.*

Chapter 1: Coastline

THIS PAGE: *The rocks at Cape Flattery, photographed during the filming for* Wings Over Washington. OPPOSITE, ABOVE: *On February 15, 1930, the Admiral Benson ran aground on Peacock Spit near the mouth of the Columbia. Here, crew members are evacuated by a rescue tram, also known as a "breeches buoy."* OPPOSITE, BELOW: *In a photograph from 1880, the remains of a shipwreck can be seen near Flattery Rocks while members of the Makah Tribe fish just offshore.*

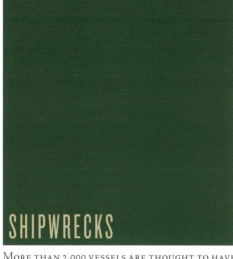

# SHIPWRECKS

More than 2,000 vessels are thought to have met their ends on reefs, shoals, sandbars, and sea stacks along the Pacific coast between Oregon's Tillamook Bay and British Columbia's Vancouver Island. The danger for captains comes in a variety of forms. The mouth of the Columbia is an ever-shifting sandbar, thanks to the combination of river flow and offshore currents, and fog and violent weather systems have also caused ships to flounder all along the coast. Peacock Spit on the north side of the river caused challenges for many ships, and was even named for one unlucky vessel—the USS *Peacock*, which ran aground there in 1841. The area around Cape Flattery can be as treacherous as the bars along the Columbia, and many vessels have been lost there in rough weather and heavy seas. In 1901 the iron steam sloop HMS *Condor* left British Columbia for Honolulu—straight into a gale at Cape Flattery. The ship never reached its destination.

In 1887 the *Austria* was headed from San Francisco to Tacoma when a gale erupted just off Cape Alava's Umatilla Reef. The ship lost several sails and the vessel was pushed shoreward, finally running aground near Cannonball Island. At very low tides the wreck of the *Austria* is still visible off the cape.

On October 4, 1893, gales blew the wood sailing vessel *Leonore* ashore at the mouth of the Quillayute River, killing the captain, his wife, and other crew members. In 1903 the *Prince Arthur* was caught in a storm, and when the crew mistook the light from a cabin on shore for a lighthouse marking the Strait of Juan de Fuca, they sailed the ship into the reef. All but two of the 20 crew aboard, most of them Norwegian apprentices, died. They were buried near the site, and today the grave is home to the Norwegian Memorial. It's no wonder the waters along the Washington coast have earned the nickname "Graveyard of the Pacific."

Chapter 1: Coastline     13

THIS PAGE: *A surfer braves the icy water of the Pacific.* OPPOSITE: *Hiking at Hole-in-the-Rock on Rialto Beach.*

## AT PLAY

Every year—late spring through late fall, come sun and blue skies or rain and fog—surfers flock to the Washington coast around Long Beach Peninsula, Westport, La Push, and Neah Bay. With cold-water swells year-round, the beaches here are lined not with surfers in board shorts and bikinis but neoprene-clad fanatics. Most breaks on the coast are shore breaks, versus reef breaks, and swells are typically largest around La Push and Westport, where they average between 5 and 15 feet.

Nearby, hikers lace up to explore the West Coast in a different way. More than 70 miles of beach stretch along the coastline within Olympic National Park, offering everything from an easy day hike to a serious multiday backpacking excursion. Families seeking adventure often head north along the coast from Rialto Beach to Hole-in-the-Wall (recognizable by the yawning O in a headland), where starfish and sea anemones fill tide pools. At high tide, however, the passage disappears and can require a steep scramble over the headlands to reach the other side.

Several miles past Hole-in-the-Wall, the coast turns to large rocky shelves, and then again to sandy beaches bordered by enormous driftwood logs. It's easy enough to camp—above the tide line—near the Chilean Memorial (and swim around sea stacks in the bay during frigid high tides) or to continue on for several miles to Cape Alava, or even Shi Shi Beach, near the Makah Reservation.

# COASTAL TRIBES

When white settlers arrived on the Washington coast, they met well-established native people. To the south, along the Columbia River and Willapa Bay were the Chinook, whose adeptness at trading stymied fur traders and Lewis and Clark. To the east lived members of the Quinault Tribe.

The Quinault people lived in permanent villages along rivers and lakes, and they harvested salmon and hunted whales and seals on the coast. In the summer, they also ventured inland to trade with other tribal groups and to hunt, often hiking into the mountain areas for game and to gather berries and plants. They carved canoes from cedar trees in sizes and designs specially adapted to swift-flowing rivers, broad estuaries, and the ocean. Farther north, the Makah hunted gray whales for thousands of years, using every part of the whale for food, to make needed items, and to trade.

Today, five Native American tribes have reservations on the shores of Washington State along the Pacific Ocean. Located in the south, on Willapa Bay near Tokeland, is the Shoalwater Bay Tribe, which includes descendants of the Willapa Chinook, Lower Chehalis, and Willapa Hills. On lush conifer forestlands, south of Olympic National Park and the Hoh Rain Forest, is the home of the Quinault Indian Nation. Nearby, the Hoh Tribe—whose people have long fished the area—has 443 acres of reservation land near Forks. The Quileute Tribe is located in La Push. And at the tip of the peninsula is Neah Bay, home of the Makah Tribe, whose prehistoric numbers are thought to be between 2,000 and 4,000 people. Today, the Makah Tribe is composed of 1,500 members, and is largely known for its whaling traditions, although a large number of tribal members make their living as visual artists.

**OPPOSITE:** *A Quileute woman is shown in a circa 1913 portrait by Edward S. Curtis.* **LEFT:** *A Chinook woman holds a gathering basket and digging stick in this circa 1910 photograph by Edward S. Curtis.* **RIGHT:** *A reproduction of a Haida longhouse features a house frontal pole, typically placed at the front of a home to portray the family's history. Although totem poles are not a traditional part of the history of Washington coast tribes, they are common among their close neighbors, the Haida of British Columbia and Tlingit of Alaska.*

# CHAPTER 2
# OLYMPIC PENINSULA

# Sun filters through mist, ferns,

and trees towering overhead to land on One Square Inch, a sanctuary of silence, considered the quietest place in the United States.

That inch is in the pristine, ecologically diverse, and largely untouched Hoh Rain Forest, deep within Olympic National Park. Designated by a red rock on a moss-covered log, the space is part of a soundscape management project designed to illuminate the sounds of nature and the beauty found in the absence of human-made noise. Three commercial airlines cooperate by rerouting planes to avoid creating noise pollution above the site. It is surrounded by the largest intact stand of coniferous forest in the contiguous 48 states. Among these trees are some of the oldest and largest in North America—massive 250-foot-tall conifers, and cedars as big around as a VW bus. Spotted owls make their home in the giant Sitka spruce and western hemlock that compete for sunlight. Elk cut through the woods. Giant yellow banana slugs edge along the forest floor.

Bounded by salt water—to the west is the Pacific Ocean, to the north is the Strait of Juan de Fuca—Olympic National Park encompasses some one million acres of forest, glacial peaks, raging rivers, and steaming hot springs. The Olympic Mountains rise within the park and across the peninsula. Their eastern slopes heave up from Puget Sound; their western slopes run toward the Pacific, where they force incoming clouds toward the mountaintops, and where the cool temperatures and low air pressure cause them to release their moisture. As a result, 12 to 14 feet of rain falls over the mountains and valleys here, creating the wettest place in the contiguous United States.

At 7,980 feet, Mount Olympus, the highest of the mountains on the peninsula, is home to eight glaciers, and towers above the other summits. Nearby, Hurricane Ridge—popular among skiers and snowboarders—rises a mile above sea level just outside the deepwater port city of Port Angeles. Home to a combination of working docks and seaside restaurants jutting over the bay, Port Angeles is also the site of the country's largest prehistoric indigenous village and burial ground found to date. Nearby, a 5.5-mile-long sand spit—the Dungeness Spit—points its way into the Strait of Juan de Fuca. Now a nature preserve with seabirds and crustaceans, the spit is also where the local crab got its name.

*Lupine on display at Mount Olympus, part of the Olympic Mountain Range.*

Farther east, lavender fields paint the valleys purple between the mountains, the forests, and the water. Set in the rain shadow of the Olympic Mountains, the area—and especially the small town of Sequim—receives a mere 16 inches of rain on average every year, much like Los Angeles, California. The resulting Mediterranean-like climate makes it perfect for raising lavender. In all, nearly 40 farms grow 110,000 plants near Sequim every year.

Perched above Puget Sound, Port Townsend looks to ferry passengers like a matchbook of homes that could plunge off the bluff and into the frigid waters at any moment. The waterfront town is known for the Victorian houses and buildings constructed during its late-19th-century heyday as well as its boat-building tradition.

Turn south from here and the waters become brackish, as glacial rivers meet the saline waters of the Pacific Ocean. Submarines ghost the waters of the Hood Canal. Tridents slip silently from their berths at Naval Base Kitsap, across from Dabob Bay, then turn toward open water. Once a World War II munitions depot, the base is now home to eight Trident submarines, and nearly 2,000 missiles. On any given day these low-hulled, 560-foot-long leviathans could be cruising silently, teasing porpoises with their underwater wake.

For 62 miles—from the northern tip of the Kitsap Peninsula to Lynch Cove near Belfair—the fishhook-shaped Hood Canal ebbs with the tides. On average, the canal is about two miles wide, and varies in depth from a maximum of 600 feet to shallow tidelands. As it snakes between the Olympic and Kitsap Peninsulas, the Hood Canal creates a perfect host environment for oysters to flourish, for wolf eels to burrow into caves, and for octopus to hunt mollusks.

**OPPOSITE:** *A view of the Olympic Mountains from Hurricane Ridge inside the Olympic National Park.*
**THIS PAGE:** *Although not native to the Olympics, mountain goats have become an iconic—and sometimes aggressive—part of the region.*

THIS PAGE: *Sunlight makes its way through the canopy of the Hoh Rain Forest.* OPPOSITE: *Emerald-green ferns and moss on the Hall of Mosses Trail in the Hoh Rain Forest.*

# ARBOREAL WONDERS

Giants rise above the earth on the Olympic Peninsula. Massive conifers, as tall as 30-story buildings, loom overhead while the Olympic yellow-pine chipmunk chatters on the verdant forest floor. Ancient Douglas firs soar more than 300 feet into the sky—more than half the height of the Space Needle's observation deck. Off Highway 101, the world's largest red cedar stands 178 feet tall and 19.4 feet in diameter and is estimated to be 1,000 years old. Near Kalaloch, between Ruby Beach and Queets, a massive 123-foot-tall, 61-foot-wide western red cedar was split in half during a 2014 storm. The largest trees in Washington are found in the valley of the Quinault Rain Forest, including the western red cedar, Sitka spruce, coastal Douglas fir, Alaska cedar, western hemlock, and mountain hemlock.

Like the coastal forests, the forests of the peninsula are filled with moss-covered logs and ferns that provide a spongy carpet layer. In the lowland forests around the Elwha River, Douglas firs provide a shaggy overhead canopy, creating a refuge for creatures of all sorts. The largest wild population of Roosevelt elk wander among junglelike rain forests festooned with trees covered in mosses and ferns and lichens. Cougars stalk dense underbrush and open rocky areas. And winged creatures such as eagles and owls nest within the forest. Once headed for extinction, the northern spotted owls nest in tree branches, hunt from their canopies late at night, and raise their young.

**OPPOSITE, ABOVE:** *Commercial fishing boats provide a picturesque tableau in Port Angeles.* **OPPOSITE, BELOW:** *Fresh produce at a market in Port Angeles.* **THIS PAGE:** *Port Angeles with the foothills of the Olympic Range in the background.*

# HIDDEN WONDERS

Waterfalls crash across the Olympic Peninsula, tumbling as much as 120 feet into the Big Quilcene River, coursing over mossy rocks near Lake Quinault, or pouring down 20 feet near Sol Duc Hot Springs. The peninsula even has its own waterfall trail map, which includes 22 falls.

Hot springs dot the peninsula, too. Within the national park are Sol Duc Hot Springs, where thermals have been incorporated into a resort, and the more remote Olympic Hot Springs. Located near the Elwha River, these natural pools vary from lukewarm to scalding and can be accessed via the Appleton Pass Trail. Along the Elwha River is the largest dam removal / river reconstruction project in US history.

Larger aquatic wonders abound in the form of Lake Quinault, deep in the Quinault Rain Forest, and the surprisingly aquamarine 624-foot-deep Lake Crescent. Formed by glaciers, the lake remains remarkably clear, thanks to water low in nitrogen, which inhibits algae growth.

Perhaps one of the greatest wonders of the peninsula and park is a result of its relative remoteness. With nearly 95 percent of the Olympic National Park designated for wilderness, natural quiet abounds.

**OPPOSITE:** *The distinctive Sol Duc Falls on the Sol Duc River.* **THIS PAGE:** *A magical spot in the rain forest close to the Sol Duc Hot Springs, a popular destination for visitors.*

THIS PAGE: *Sunset casts Hood Canal in pink and purple.* OPPOSITE, ABOVE: *One of the many waterfowl found on Hood Canal: a harlequin duck.* OPPOSITE, BELOW: *A Trident submarine churns through the waters of Hood Canal near Naval Base Kitsap-Bangor.*

# TRAILWORTHY

From mountain biking to hiking to skiing, the Olympic Peninsula offers some amazing trails. Skiers at Hurricane Ridge Ski and Snowboard Area can drop in for a run among these glades and bowls within the national park.

Mountain biking is a huge sport on the peninsula, thanks in part to the Olympic National Forest, which nearly surrounds the national park and which promotes the sport. From steep tracks to narrow gravel roads, hundreds of trails crisscross the forest. Mount Muller Trail near Forks starts in lush forest and climbs 3,200 feet to a ridge offering views of Mount Olympus, Lake Crescent, and the Strait of Juan de Fuca. And the Skokomish Lower South Fork Trail meanders along rivers peppered with fishermen.

With more than 75 miles of Pacific coast, 600 lakes, and 4,000 miles of rivers and streams, the region is very popular for fishing. Countless boats depart docks across the peninsula for deep-sea fishing, too.

Hiking is king on the peninsula. On the Strait of Juan de Fuca, explore the Dungeness Spit on a seven-mile round-trip walk along the Olympic Discovery Trail to the Dungeness National Wildlife Refuge. Hikes in the area range from easy day hikes, such as along the Duckabush River Trail, which laces through an ancient forest, to serious climbs. Those who prefer to summit can ascend 3,580 feet from Glacier Meadows to reach the summit of Mount Olympus within Olympic National Park in just four to six miles.

**LEFT AND RIGHT:** *Mountain bikers dazzle on a trail in the Olympic National Forest, a popular haven for the sport.*

# CHAPTER 3

# PUGET SOUND

# HARBOR SEALS, SPOTTED GRAY AND

glistening, pry mussels from pilings. Sixgill sharks swim in deep water as sea lions fin past ferries, and octopuses jet the deeps, changing from red to purple as they go.

Puget Sound, an inlet of the Pacific Ocean contained wholly within the Salish Sea, stretches 100 miles from Olympia in the south to Deception Pass at the northern end of Whidbey Island. The waters are 450 feet deep on average—and cold, the perfect environment for a wild array of marine life. The giant Pacific octopus—the world's largest octopus—makes its home here, as do bald eagles, gray whales, orcas, and more than 200 species of fish.

South of where Nisqually River delta floodplains meet Puget Sound stands the state capitol, Olympia, with its views of the Olympic Mountains. The area has been home to Lushootseed-speaking peoples, such as the Squaxin, Nisqually, Puyallup, Chehalis, Suquamish, and Duwamish, for thousands of years. Today, it is home to the governor's mansion and the Washington State legislative building, which is topped by a 287-foot-high wooden dome.

Follow Puget Sound north from here, and the water moves between islands and inlets large and small. The Tacoma Narrows Bridge is formed from twin suspensions and connects the mainland to Gig Harbor, Bremerton, and beyond by spanning the Narrows, the strait separating the Kitsap Peninsula and Tacoma. Beneath the bridge, a tidal current surges river-like as it gushes through the Narrows. To the east is blue-collar, industrious Tacoma, with its working seaport, shuttered paper mills, Chihuly's stunning *Bridge of Glass*, and one of the world's largest wooden domed structures, the Tacoma Dome. To the west lies the Kitsap Peninsula, laced with ports and harbors, lakes and inlets.

Vashon Island lies on the southwest side of the Sound. This hilly, bucolic, farm-covered island is also a ferry-served bedroom community of Seattle. Hills covered in apple orchards roll down into forests and up again to offer views of the water, of Seattle to the northeast, and the Tacoma Narrows to the south.

*Waves wash over gravely sand at Picnic Point State Park in Snohomish County.*

Across the water to the northwest is 28-square-mile Bainbridge Island. For thousands of years, the Suquamish Tribe hunted and foraged the fertile lands. By the late 1800s, after the first Europeans arrived, Port Blakely was the world's largest sawmill. By the early 1900s, the island was covered in strawberry fields and a thriving, integrated community of immigrants. The Japanese American community flourished here until 1942, when the government interred 275 men, women, and children—two-thirds of them US citizens—removing them to crude camps in Idaho or the deserts of California. After the war ended three years later, 150 people returned. Today, the island is home to gardens and wineries, an arts museum, a memorial to the Japanese Americans interred, and a native history museum.

Nearby, on the Kitsap Peninsula, is Bremerton. Naval destroyers and aircraft carriers dominate the coastline, thanks to the nation's sixth-largest naval base, Naval Base Kitsap—a 2004 merger of Naval Station Bremerton and Naval Submarine Base Bangor. The base is connected to the Puget Sound Naval Shipyard, established in 1891. Today, it features four nuclear shipyards, a strategic nuclear weapons facility, an aircraft carrier handling dry dock, and an enormous fuel depot.

To the east of Vashon and Bainbridge Islands is the state's biggest city, Seattle. North of Seattle is the port town of Everett, which is home to the Boeing assembly plant, where jumbo jets course down runways and in and out of enormous hangars. The

**OPPOSITE:** *The Bloedel Reserve, located on Bainbridge Island, is a 150-acre public garden that blends formal gardens with natural woodlands and native Pacific Northwest plantings.* **ABOVE:** *Reefnetting for salmon off Lummi Island. Reefnetting is a traditional Native American fishing method still practiced by tribal members in the Pacific Northwest.* **BELOW:** *The Port of Kingston.*

Chapter 3: Puget Sound

plant is the world's largest building (by volume). There, 747s, 767s, 777s, and the new 787 line of aircraft are being built. Nearby is Tulalip Bay, surrounded by the Tulalip Reservation, which was established for members of the Snohomish, Snoqualmie, Skykomish, and other allied tribes.

North along Puget Sound, more islands rise from the water. At about 55 miles north to south, Whidbey Island is full of rolling pastures and fields and dotted with artist colonies and small-town fishing communities. At its boomeranged waist is the town of Coupeville, which straddles the mussel-growing waters of Penn Cove. Once home to three Lower Skagit tribe villages, Penn Cove's protected harbor offers an abundance of salmon, clams, mussels, flounder, and sole as well as easy access to nearby waterways and inland forests. Churning Deception Pass lies beyond the island's curve. Below the Pass's rocky cliffs, which stand roughly 400 feet above the tide, eddies roll and waves stand on end as tidal exchanges collide, causing whirlpools to roil between Fidalgo and Whidbey Islands.

The Washington State Ferry system, which serves Puget Sound and the San Juan Islands, is the nation's largest, servicing on average more than 23 million riders every year on 10 different routes. Several routes provide the opportunity for island dwellers to commute to Seattle daily for work (and pleasure), including ferries that connect Bremerton, Bainbridge Island, and Vashon Island with Seattle.

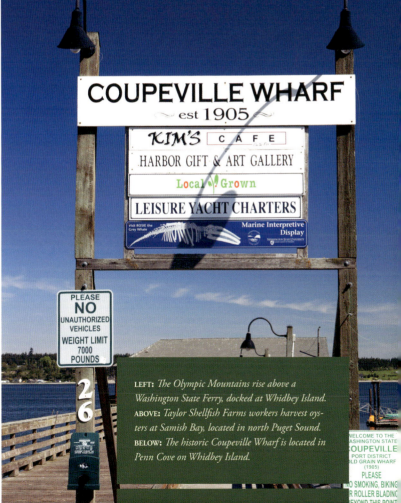

**LEFT:** *The Olympic Mountains rise above a Washington State Ferry, docked at Whidbey Island.*
**ABOVE:** *Taylor Shellfish Farms workers harvest oysters at Samish Bay, located in north Puget Sound.*
**BELOW:** *The historic Coupeville Wharf is located in Penn Cove on Whidbey Island.*

**THIS PAGE:** *The two-span Deception Pass Bridge connects Whidbey Island to Fidalgo Island.*
**NEXT SPREAD, ABOVE LEFT:** *Harbor seals are one of the diverse species of sea life in the Puget Sound.*
**NEXT SPREAD, BELOW LEFT:** *The giant Pacific octopus is the largest octopus in the world. It is commonly seen by divers at popular diving spots in the Sound.*
**NEXT SPREAD, RIGHT:** *Orcas are familiar denizens of the Puget Sound. The members of the J, K, and L pods are local celebrities.*

## INTO THE DEEP

There's a reason Jacques Cousteau loved the Pacific Northwest. The cold waters here attract amazing creatures. Salmon, steelhead trout, and enormous cod swim alongside sea lions, sea otters, gray whales, humpback whales, and orcas. There are also sharks. Spiny dogfish, broadnose sevengills, and brown catsharks roam these waters, as does the amazing bluntnose sixgill shark, with an average length of 16 feet.

On the ocean floor, sea anemones sway and sunflower sea stars bloom in a rainbow of colors. Moon jellies ghost past, almost transparent, trailing tentacles that inject poison, while blunt-faced wolf eels, with their razor-sharp teeth, dart their pouty faces from rocky caves to hunt sea urchins and passing prey. Nearby, red-brown giant Pacific octopuses cavort, growing to 90 pounds on average.

## PORTS OF CALL

In 1852 a water-powered sawmill was constructed on Commencement Bay, and the South Sound was forever changed. Tacoma grew in the shadow of Mount Rainier, becoming the terminus for the Northern Pacific Railroad, and soon grain terminals and warehouses lined the waterway. The city boomed during World War I with its lumber-fed shipyards on the tidal flats, and today the port bustles with cargo. Comprising the Northwest Seaport Alliance, the ports of Tacoma and Seattle make up the third-largest container gateway in the United States, the two ports together are the third-largest container gateway in the United States.

Founded in 1891, the city of Bremerton is a different kind of working port. Home to the Puget Sound Naval Shipyard, the city attracted the attention of the US Navy, thanks to its sheltered bay and access to deep waters. The US warship *Oregon* was the first battleship to dock at the naval shipyard in 1897.

The navy yard's mission changed in 1916, as a result of World War I, from that of overhaul and repair to construction of new ships. During the last year of World War I the yard built two minesweepers and ammunition ships, seven submarines, seven seagoing tugboats, 25 submarine chasers, and 1,700 small boats.

Due to the yard's location in the Pacific amphitheater, five of the American warships damaged during the Pearl Harbor attack of World War II were sent to the shipyard for repairs.

42     Wings Over Washington

*In the early 1900s, Tacoma was known as the lumber capital of America. In this circa 1925 photograph, lumber is stacked for export.*

Chapter 3: Puget Sound

**THIS PAGE:** *Kiteboarding has become an increasingly popular sport in the region for good reason: plenty of wind and water.* **OPPOSITE, ABOVE:** *Sport fishermen fish from a pier with the Seattle skyline in the background.* **OPPOSITE, BELOW:** *Breezy days find sailors on the Puget Sound in anything from one-man dinghies to crewed yachts.*

## SOUND SPORTS

Pacific Northwesterners love their sports, especially those on the water. Everett's narrow Jetty Island—which offers a long spit of pretty sand, access to the waters and winds of Puget Sound, and close proximity to Seattle—attracts kiteboarders in droves all summer long, while scuba divers regularly explore the pilings and docks around Alki Beach in Seattle and off Vashon Island, as well as the Edmonds Underwater Park, which is home to massive lingcod.

Boats of all sizes decorate Puget Sound year-round, particularly in summer when fishermen (and fisherwomen) reel in salmon and flounder and drag in crab pots heavy with Dungeness crabs. Paddleboarders coast along the waters of Seattle's Elliott Bay around Alki and north of downtown in Shilshole Bay. And the waters here sprout brightly colored sails spring through fall as sailboats race between the islands and up and down Puget Sound.

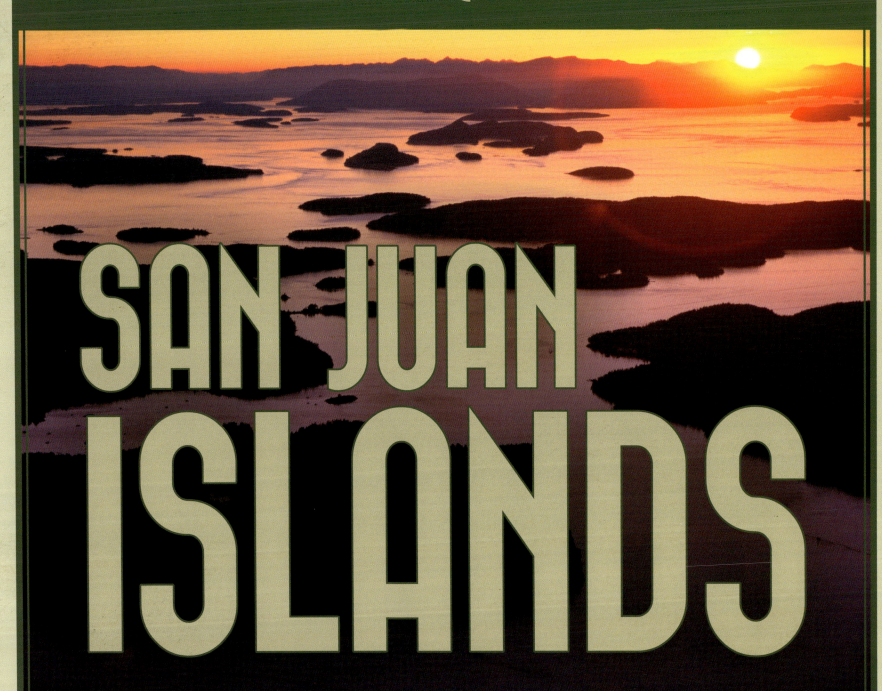

CHAPTER 4

SAN JUAN ISLANDS

# AN ARCHIPELAGO BEGINS IN THE WATERS

just north of the Strait of Juan de Fuca and south of the open waters of the Strait of Georgia. Bedrock islands jut out of the salty Salish Sea and are covered in wetlands and madrona trees, cedars, and pine forests. These are the San Juan Islands, where more than 740 rocks, reefs, and islands can appear at low tide, although only 172 of the reefs and islands are named.

Even the tiniest isles—ones that seem to drift in the middle of a channel—can provide hours of adventure when you're gunkholing these waters. And that's what gunkholing is: the art of meandering in and out of bays and coves, dropping anchor—and crab pots and fishing lines—into the inky depths along the way. These waters teem with marine life. Gray whales, humpbacks, and harbor porpoises swim through the inlets; eagles and cormorants wing overhead. The islands' waters are lush with more than 80 orca whales that live in communities of mothers and their offspring. These communities—the J, K, and L pods—make the waters here their summer home. In winter, when salmon become more scarce in the cold northern waters, these mammals, also known as killer whales, typically travel south along the Pacific coast in search of easy food. Come spring, the tuxedoed creatures return to the waters of the San Juans.

The Lummi, Samish, and other Northern Straits Coast Salish people made the islands home for thousands of years. Artifacts such as shell middens, tools, and artificial reefs suggest that the area has been inhabited for more than 9,000 years, with recent archeological discoveries indicating that some settlers reached the islands at least 14,000 years ago—soon after the Ice Age glaciers receded. For various reasons, by the late 1700s, the Northern Straits Salish had begun leaving their winter villages on the islands for mainland sites, returning in summer to fish, garden, and collect shellfish.

A mere handful of the islands in the San Juans are inhabited, and four are accessible by state ferry: San Juan Island, Orcas Island, Lopez Island, and Shaw Island. In summer they teem with cyclists, sailors, and tourists. In winter, the population returns to local farmers, craftspeople, service workers artists, and a fair number of telecommuters. The islands

*A pod of orcas swim off San Juan Island.*

THIS PAGE: *The night sky from San Juan Island.* RIGHT, ABOVE: *Waves sweep over the rocky coast on Lopez Island.* RIGHT, BELOW: *A San Juan Island barn.* OPPOSITE: *Cattle Point Lighthouse is found on the southernmost point of San Juan Island.*

are dappled in sunlight year-round—benefiting from the rain shadow effect of nearby mountains and seeing less than half the rain that Seattle does every year, and averaging more than 240 days of sunshine. By night, the stars appear in breathtaking patterns overhead while bioluminescent creatures give off a green glow in disturbed waters.

On Lopez Island, rolling farmlands give way to sandy beaches. With its relative flatness, ample pastureland, and bucolic scenery, Lopez attracts recreational cyclists. Just 15 miles long, the island refers to itself as "The Friendly Isle," based in large part on the local custom of motorists waving as they pass one another. Come Saturdays in summer, a farmers market hums with life as local vendors sell island-grown garlic, melon, Lopez lamb, and farmstead goat cheese, alongside potters and jewelers. Here, too, are historic barns and farmhouses, as well as a historic water tower and pump house that is more than 100 years old.

At San Juan Island's Friday Harbor, kayaks wind past sailboats at anchor as seaplanes taxi in to dock. Onshore, a waterfront park stands at the edge of a historic one-square-mile downtown. Established by the Hudson's Bay Company in the mid-1800s, Friday Harbor was once home to salmon-curing stations and sheep farms. Today, the town is full of galleries and restaurants, museums and wildlife-tour operators. At the other side of the island, a 19-acre, 120-piece sculpture park welcomes visitors to the resort town of Roche Harbor. The island offers up fields of lavender and beaches as well as rocky, lighthouse-capped harbors.

Ferries ply the waters around San Juan Island, delivering cars and passengers to Orcas Island, where artist studios and apple barns line rural roads that dip through old-growth forests. In town, shellfish farms and galleries stud former fishing villages such as Eastsound. At opposite ends of the island's upside-down U shape are the hamlets of Deer Harbor, with its sandy beach, and Doe Bay, near Moran State Park, with its resort and annual music festival. Also here, on the eastern side of the island, rises Mount Constitution, with its ice-blue mountain lake and stunning Cascade Range views.

Nearby is tiny Shaw Island, just under eight square miles in size. The island is home to a monastery of Benedictine nuns, and for 27 years, until 2004, the Franciscan Sisters of the Eucharist ran the island's general store and operated the ferry landing. Shaw is also home to the state's longest-running, continually used schoolhouse. Built in 1890, the historic Little Red Schoolhouse serves elementary and middle school students and is still considered a one-room schoolhouse, although the addition of a computer center did technically expand it to two rooms.

While Shaw, Orcas, Lopez, and San Juan Islands are all serviced by the Washington State Ferry system, private, passenger-only ferries service other smaller nearby islands, such as Lummi, Eliza, Sinclair, and Blakely Islands.

**OPPOSITE:** *Sucia Island is the largest of a ten-island archipelago. The cluster of tiny islands makes up the Sucia Island State Park.* **THIS PAGE:** *Shells scattered on the beach on Shaw Island's Blind Bay.*

*The view from Mount Constitution on Orcas Island. Mount Constitution is the highest point in the San Juan Islands.*

## SCENIC BYWAY

The three-segment San Juan Islands Scenic Byway is among the more unusual routes in the United States. The first 30 miles must be traveled by water via the Washington State Ferries that connect the islands to the mainland. Once ashore, the byway picks up on San Juan Island, where it traces through Friday Harbor and into American Camp and San Juan Island National Historical Park. On the west side of the island it passes English Camp, reaching at last the marina town of Roche Harbor. On Orcas, the byway laces along the horseshoe-shaped island to stop at quaint villages and roadside artist studios, swimmable Cascade Lake and hikable Mount Constitution, as well as the 80-acre forest park at the southeastern tip of the island, Obstruction Pass State Park.

# THE UNUSUAL JUANS

There's something about island life that inspires a different take on things. In the San Juans that means everything from a war over a single pig to bootlegging.

San Juan Island National Historical Park commemorates the "Pig War" between the United States and the British Empire, in which the only casualty was a large black hog. The Pig War is the common name for a 13-year standoff that began in 1859 when an American settler shot an Irishman's pig on the island that both countries claimed. It resulted in only the one porcine death, but led to the creation of San Juan County and the final borders that define Washington today.

Not far away, at the Ryan family farm, pyramids of salt are forming slowly under hoop houses. The San Juan Island Sea Salt company harnesses the sun's evaporative powers on ponds of seawater under plastic-covered greenhouses, of a sort, to make the artisan salt.

Friday Harbor is home to the Center for Whale Research and The Whale Museum, which houses real whale skeletons. There is also a sighting map, where San Juan's most famous residents are tracked. Nearby, Lime Kiln State Park is one of the best places in the world to view whales. Thanks to the unique hydrographic properties of the site, onshore visitors can be within 20 feet of breaching whales.

Smuggling flourished in the islands starting in the mid-1800s because taxes and import duties weren't collected due to the US and British joint occupation. Later, the islands were used to smuggle opium, silk, and Canadian wool, as well as Chinese workers into the United States following the Chinese Exclusion Act of 1882. In the 1920s, Prohibition offered a new money-spinning field for rumrunners in the islands, who evaded revenue agents as they smuggled alcohol from Canada to the United States.

On the more demure side of things, Shaw Island is the smallest of the islands serviced by ferry, and it's also home to a Benedictine convent. At the Our Lady of the Rock Monastery, the contemplative order of nuns farm, run a raw milk dairy, and carry out eight daily prayer services and mass in Gregorian chant.

OPPOSITE: *Lime Kiln Lighthouse is considered one of the world's best places for orca viewing, with the whales frequently passing close to shore.* THIS PAGE: *A nun from Our Lady of the Rock Monastery on Shaw Island tends a flower garden.*

## ACTIVE LIFE, ISLAND STYLE

Arguably the islands' best hike is to the top of 2,409-foot Mount Constitution with its views east to the mainland's Cascade Range, north to Mount Baker near the Canada border, and even south to Mount Rainier. The moderate seven-mile round-trip trek starts at the shores of Mountain Lake in Orcas Island's Moran State Park.

A wooded 80-acre nature preserve surrounds Hummel Lake near Lopez Village and on the other side of the island, a hike to the 470-foot summit of Chadwick Hill on Watmough Bay offers up views over Rosario Strait to Whidbey Island. For views on San Juan Island, there's the hike up Mount Finlayson, where a wide trail leads through an evergreen forest to deliver the summit and views of the Juan de Fuca Strait, the Olympic Mountains, and Vancouver Island.

Cyclists love Lopez Island, with its interwoven beaches and forests and gently rolling farmlands, and the more rigorous San Juan Island with its 43 miles of challenging loops and legs. Orcas Island is full of narrow winding roads, steep grades, and even the chance to climb to the top of 2,409-foot Mount Constitution.

Kayakers flock to San Juan waters to explore seemingly hidden reefs and to hug calm shorelines while still skimming over the exceptionally deep waters where orcas pass by. Sailors, meanwhile, can race the winds for hours, circling entire islands as porpoises jump in the distance.

**LEFT:** *Kayaking is a popular sport in the San Juans, allowing recreationists a water-level view of the islands.* **ABOVE AND BELOW:** *Friday Harbor, located on San Juan Island, is the only incorporated town in the San Juans.*

**THIS PAGE AND OPPOSITE:** *With its historic resort and protected harbor, Roche Harbor is a popular and picturesque destination.*

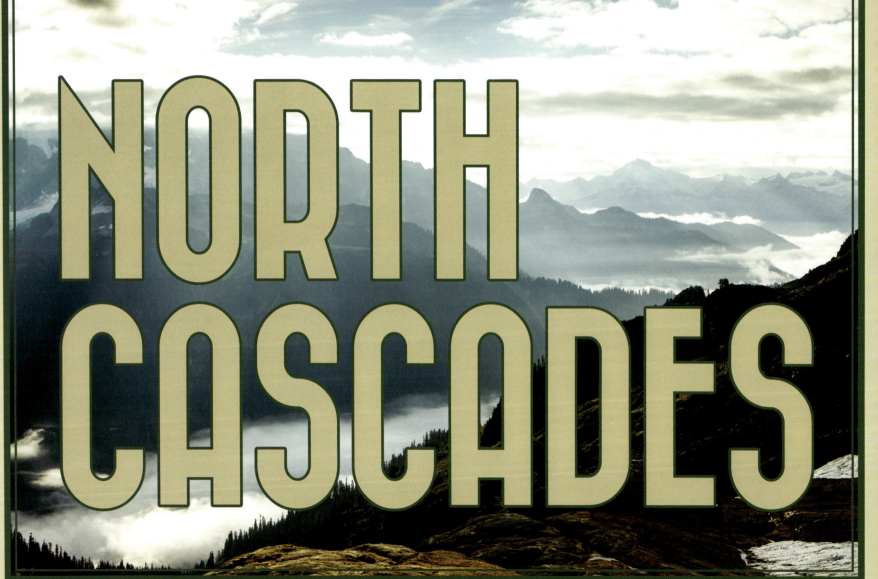

# CHAPTER 5

# NORTH CASCADES

# TULIPS FLUTTER IN VIBRANT COLORS

across black earth, flagging the farmland from edge to edge. Deep in the heart of Skagit Valley, farms and orchards dot the landscape, but it is the 300 acres of tulips that captivate. The Skagit River, flowing out of British Columbia into Ross Lake and through the valley, further nourishes fertile lands and provides spawning habitat for all five native salmon species.

North of the valley, the fields turn to foothills until roads wind high along forest ridges. Below the craggy tree-lined cliffs of Chuckanut Drive, Bellingham Bay ebbs and recedes, revealing tidal flats rich with oyster farms and wildlife. Surf smelt spawn on the beaches, pelagic cormorants spread their wings in the sun, and great blue herons hunt the shoreline.

Just south of the Canada border sits Bellingham, a college town and seaport, where old brick buildings rise near the working port that hosts ferry traffic headed for Alaska. The city is home to Western Washington University. Established in 1886 as a teaching college for women, in the 1960s it founded the nation's first environmental science college. Today, WWU educates more than 15,000 students a year on 215 acres south of downtown.

Turn east and snow drifts across mountain peaks and eagles soar above icy rivers. Especially in winter, massive bald eagles congregate along the North Fork Nooksack River to hunt spawning salmon.

Washington State Route 20, also known as the North Cascades Highway, winds east through forest and into the Cascade Range, which begins in British Columbia and ends in northern California. It slinks past Ross Lake—spread out blue as a robin egg—then delivers a stunning view of a cluster of 7,500-tall granite spires known as the Liberty Bell massif.

**ABOVE:** *When salmon spawn in the Skagit River, eagles descend on the Skagit Valley, waiting to feast on their carcasses.* **BELOW:** *Cotton-candy tulips in a field in the Skagit Valley. Tulips have been grown in the region since 1906.*

THIS PAGE: *A kayaker glides by far below a madrona tree in Chuckanut Bay near Bellingham.* OPPOSITE: *A wintry view of Mount Shuksan in the Cascade Mountains. Lake Ann is in the foreground.*

To the south, the Cascades turn into volcanic uplifts. In the steep, rugged North Cascades, though, snow and glaciers dominate, although it also has its own volcanoes, including two of the five major volcanoes in Washington, Mount Baker and Glacier Peak. In fact, in summer, photographers flock to Mount Shuksan to shoot the peak and its mirror image in Picture Lake, but come winter, skiers and snowboarders throng nearby Mount Baker Ski Area. There is so much snow within this stretch of the mountains that accumulations of up to 1,000 inches are common, and the ski resort itself set the world record for snowfall—95 feet—during the winter of 1998–1999.

Snow gathers in ribbons, packs deep into crevasses, and shifts between subalpine stands of trees. Deep in the heart of the mountains, within North Cascades National Park, glaciers form and recede, and more are found here than anywhere else in the nation outside of Alaska.

Farther on, near the top of the pass, the Pacific Crest Trail dips into the park near the 7,000-foot elevation level, then runs south over 5,392-foot Cascade Pass, to where hikers can drop into Stehekin, the tiny town (about 75 permanent residents) on the end of Lake Chelan that is accessible only by floatplane, by ferry, or on foot.

East of North Cascades National Park, and north of Lake Chelan, the Methow River snakes its way out of the mountains through Douglas fir and ponderosa pine near the town of Mazama. It curls into the frontier town of Winthrop, once a destination for gold miners and trappers. Today, the town revels in its past with its 1890s-style Old West storefronts, wooden boardwalks, and the oldest legal saloon in Washington State.

The river runs are dappled with fishermen angling for steelhead and trout. River otters cavort in the cold waters, and wolves, cougars, mountain lions, mule deer, and bear hunt and forage on the river's shores. From here, the river carves its way into Twisp and through the Okanagan's pine forests and wildlands until at last it greets the Columbia River.

**OPPOSITE:** *The Methow River meanders through the North Cascades.* **THIS PAGE:** *The Old West town of Winthrop is known for its original buildings and historical recreations.*

Chapter 5: North Cascades

*Ross, Diablo, and Gorge Lakes were created by a series of dams on the Skagit River. Shown here is the view from Ross Lake Overlook.*

A massive lake also drains into the Methow River near the tourist town of Chelan; it is the largest natural lake in the state. Carved by glaciers, Lake Chelan stretches an azure 50.5 miles to disappear into the Cascade Mountains. The lake is narrow, deep, and cold, with a maximum depth of 1,400 feet and the deepest bottom some 400 feet below sea level. It is surrounded by orchards and farmland, and increasingly by vineyards where white wine grapes flourish in the hilly terrain.

To the south, the Bavarian-style village of Leavenworth seems perfectly situated among the craggy peaks of Washington. Reinvented to feature a Bavarian theme in 1962, the town has shops brimming with lederhosen and cured meats, restaurants fronted by Tudor detailing, and wurst gardens galore, all of which are set above cold, stony Icicle Creek and below soaring peaks reminiscent of the Alps.

Chapter 5: North Cascades

THIS PAGE: *Ice climbing on Mount Baker.* OPPOSITE: *The Pacific Coast Trail transverses the Methow Pass.*

# THE PACIFIC CREST TRAIL

The Pacific Crest Trail (PCT) extends 2,650 miles from southern California at the Mexico border through Oregon and Washington to the Canada border. Five hundred of those miles are within Washington State. From the south, the trail climbs through Gifford Pinchot National Forest and the Mount Adams Wilderness, and into Mount Rainier National Park, then over Snoqualmie Pass and Stevens Pass before entering Lake Chelan National Recreation Area, where hikers can leave the trail for a stay in Stehekin, on the northwest end of Lake Chelan.

In the North Cascades, the trail repeats climbs from deep canyons to high mountain passes. The PCT also passes the Alpine Lakes Wilderness and Glacier Peak Wilderness—with its rugged, roller-coaster switchbacks—and enters North Cascades National Park. This part of the North Cascades, known as Section K, has the reputation of being both the most rugged, thanks to those extensive switchbacks and repeated climbs and descents, and the wettest. This route lies within a storm track most of the year, and precipitation in the area contributes to the massive glaciers of the national park.

The Washington section of the PCT has multiple high passes and ridges, including the highest just south of the Canada border, Lakeview Ridge. At 7,126 feet elevation, the area is home to Alaska cedar and grand fir as well as deciduous Western larch.

**OPPOSITE:** *Apple orchards on the bank of Lake Chelan.* **THIS PAGE:** *Lake Chelan is framed by fruit orchards in the foreground and the Cascade Mountains behind.*

## HIT THE TRAIL

In the Methow Valley, the nation's largest cross-country skiing trail system stretches 120 miles through high desert and rolling hills and past gurgling rivers. In winter, the Methow Community Trail connects four Nordic ski trail systems and includes a suspension bridge over the Methow River, and multiple trailside lodges. Come summer these trails teem with equestrians, bikers, and hikers seeking wildflower meadows and ascents into North Cascades National Park.

Nearby, rock climbers swarm to great climbing routes among sharp granite peaks in the North Cascades, including Liberty Bell Mountain. Here, along the North Cascades Highway one mile south of Washington Pass, climbers ascend some 18 routes, including Liberty Crack, which is considered one of the 50 classic climbs in North America.

OPPOSITE: *A climber navigates the Beckey Route on Liberty Bell Mountain.* THIS PAGE: *Fresh snow at Mount Shuksan awaits a cross-country skier.*

CHAPTER 5: NORTH CASCADES

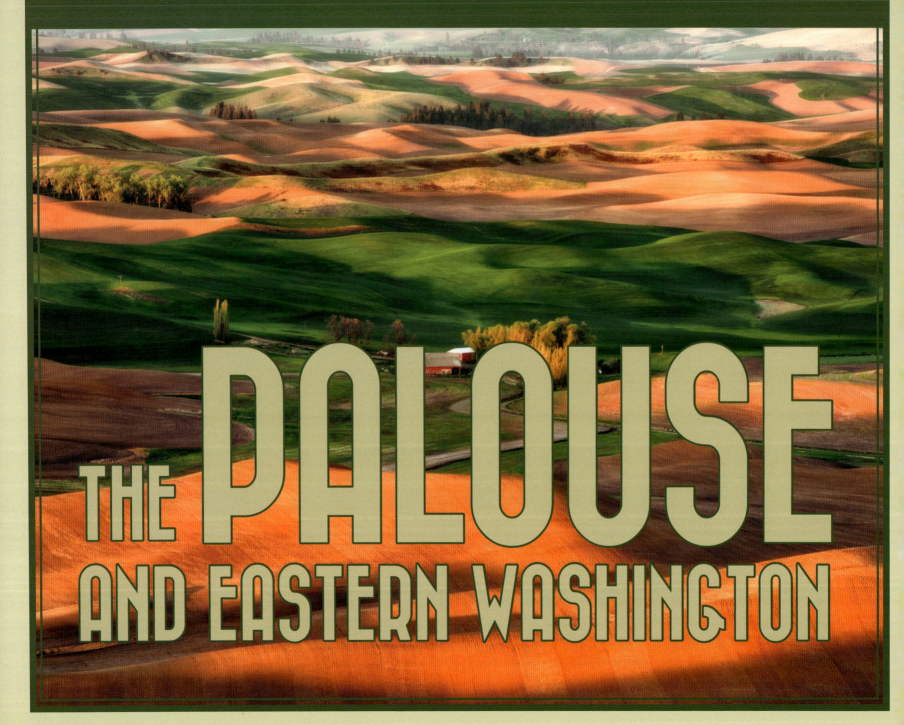

# WHEAT ROLLS IN SHIMMERING GREEN

waves across the eastern Washington plains. The effect is otherworldly, as if a grass-colored ocean has moved in on the land. As far as the eye can see, verdant fields billow beneath sunny blue skies and across a seemingly endless procession of hills, turning golden once fall arrives.

Stretching from the Oregon border to the Canada border, the eastern edge of Washington is stunning in its geographic diversity. To the north the Colville National Forest lands include the largest growth of virgin forest—western red cedar and Douglas fir, grand fir and larch—left in eastern Washington. Massive lakes and dams punctuate desert landscapes to the east. Wild horses roam eastern prairies where miles of some of the nation's most fertile farmlands meld into mountain steppes.

It is no wonder the Palouse is one of the most photographed places in the world. Photographers visit here spring through fall to catch the fields in all their glory under bright blue skies. They arrive for the charm of red barns along quiet highways, grain elevators rising above the fields in small towns like Oakesdale, or to see the vintage neon signs displayed in the Mayberry-esque town of Pomeroy.

At the southern end of the region, the Snake River notches its way through limestone plateaus to form Hells Canyon, the deepest river gorge in North America. In places, the river surges more than a mile below the canyon's west rim. Beyond the canyon the river curves south into Oregon and west to where it meets the Columbia at Pasco.

North of the Snake River, those farmlands tumble in green fields of wheat and legumes toward the college town of Pullman, home of Washington State University and the Cougars football team. Named for George Pullman, industrialist and inventor of the sleeping car, the town is situated atop four major hills and along the Palouse River, surrounded by fields of lentils, chickpeas, wheat, and peas.

About 15 miles east of Pullman in Uniontown, a fence of more than 1,000 wagon and tractor wheels encircles a former dairy barn turned arts center. To the west of Pullman, mostly hidden between rocky buttes and high-desert mesas, courses a tributary of the Snake River—the Palouse River, which winds for 167 miles between sagebrush and desert, unseen from afar until it emerges at an ancient waterfall. Framed by cathedrals of stone, Palouse Falls tumbles some 198 feet between basalt monoliths into a deep, dark pool.

*Agriculture remains a way of life in many parts of the Palouse and eastern Washington.*

THIS PAGE: *The Lower Spokane Falls in the business district of the city of Spokane.* OPPOSITE: *The spectacular Palouse Falls is Washington State's official waterfall.*

Washington State's second-largest city, Spokane, rises out of the plains in the east. Given its location at the edge of the basaltic Channeled Scablands steppe, where the landscape can be barren and full of craters and basalt outcroppings, the approach to the Lilac City can be wild with sagebrush, all of which make the city itself a verdant surprise. Located southwest of the Selkirk Mountains, which are said to be even older than the nearby Rocky Mountains, Spokane is intersected by a cascading series of waterfalls, lined with one of the nation's most scenic urban parks, and lush with Romanesque Revival–style buildings. Spokane is also home to Gonzaga University and the Bulldogs basketball team.

East of Spokane lies an enormous man-made lake. Where the mighty Grand Coulee Dam pens in the Columbia River, it forms the 130-mile-long Franklin D. Roosevelt Lake. There are more than 1,100 dams in the state, but the Coulee is by far the grandest. It is also the largest electric power–producing facility in the United States. Standing 550 feet tall and 5,223 feet

THIS PAGE: *Kettle Falls was a traditional fishing and gathering spot for the tribes of the area. The falls were flooded when the Columbia River was dammed.* OPPOSITE: *The view of Banks Lake from Steamboat Rock. The reservoir was created by Grand Coulee Dam.*

wide, the gravity-fed dam produces enough kilowatt hours of electric to supply 2.3 million homes annually. Its reservoir, Lake Roosevelt, supplies water for the irrigation of 671,000 acres. The creation of the dam flooded 21,000 acres of land, including Kettle Falls, a vital salmon fishing and meeting site for many indigenous tribes of Washington.

Over the mere 110 miles that separate Spokane from the Canada border to the north, the landscape turns green with pines as it enters the Colville National Forest, where the snow-capped mountains of the Okanagan, Kettle River, and Selkirk ranges pierce the horizon, and the last remaining herd of caribou in the Lower 48 roams among old-growth forests.

Chapter 6: The Palouse

THIS PAGE: *The distinctive fall coloring of western larch.* OPPOSITE, ABOVE: *A herd of caribou in the Colville National Forest.* OPPOSITE, BELOW: *Tufted phlox and ponderosa pinecones.*

## COUGARS OF THE EASTERN PLAINS

At the heart of Pullman is Washington's only land-grant university, Washington State University—or "Wazzu." The Cougars' campus is also home to one incredible creamery, Ferdinand's, which produces both gourmet ice cream and award-winning cheese; Martin Stadium; the Lewis Alumni Centre—a former beef cattle barn renovated as the most luxurious building on campus; and the 7,305-yard Palouse Ridge championship golf course.

WSU is also known for its veterinary program—the only one of its kind in Washington State—as well as its wild-animal research. At the School of the Environment's Bear Research, Education, and Conservation Center, students study the nutrition and behavior of grizzly bears, among other things. During nonhibernating months, the center's captive bears can be seen from a viewing center.

Art thrives here in the Palouse, too. Unbeknownst to many, WSU's Museum of Art is home to 174 prints and photographs by Andy Warhol and 206 prints by pop artist Jim Dine.

OPPOSITE, ABOVE: *Western State University fans cheer for the Cougs.* OPPOSITE, BELOW: *Greetings at the entrance to the WSU campus.* THIS PAGE: *A sweeping view toward the town of Pullman and the WSU campus taken from the Kamiak Butte.*

## ROLL ON

Wheat fields aren't the only things that roll into the distance in eastern Washington. A string of biking trails also laces the region. The seven-mile Bill Chipman Palouse Trail links Pullman to Moscow, Idaho. It also connects to the Latah Trail, which travels over 12 miles to Troy, Idaho. To the north, the 37-mile paved Spokane River Centennial Trail extends from Nine Mile Falls to the Washington and Idaho border, passing through the Spokane and Liberty Lake region as it goes.

Golf reigns in the region, too. Near Spokane are adjacent courses Liberty Lake and MeadowWood. The former offers recently renovated tree-lined fairways, 14 bunkers, and one lake, and the latter offers Robert Muir Graves–designed links-style play, deep bunkers, and tricky doglegs. In Pullman, on the WSU campus, Palouse Ridge offers distracting views of Idaho's Moscow Mountain while making use of the dramatic natural landscape, including features such as native fescue grasses and pine trees.

There's also jet boating and whitewater rafting. Tour operators abound to take whitewater enthusiasts into the rapids of Hells Canyon to skirt basalt columns and roll over standing waves. Rocky Mountain bighorn sheep, mountain goats, deer, and elk graze along the river as its passengers float beneath towering sandstone cliffs.

Fishing is quite popular in the region as well. Trout, bass, and sometimes even 10-foot-long white sturgeon can be found swimming the waters of the Snake River. The Grande Ronde, which merges with the Snake River, is one of the nation's finest steelhead streams from September to early April. In summer the river turns into a haven for smallmouth bass, rainbow trout, and channel catfish.

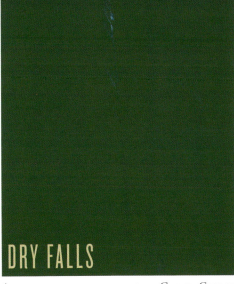

## DRY FALLS

About 20 miles south of the Grand Coulee Dam stands the remains of an immense former waterfall. Carved by ice-age floods, the now-dry cliff is 400 feet high and 3.5 miles wide.

The falls were created when catastrophic flooding channeled water at a speed of 65 miles per hour through the Upper Grand Coulee and over the tall rock face. The flow of the falls was estimated to be 10 times the current flow of all the rivers in the world combined. Later, large plunge pools at the base of Dry Falls were created when Lake Missoula flooded parts of Washington under hundreds of feet of water in just a few days.

Today the water must be imagined, but the cliffs that remain are viewable from within the Sun Lakes–Dry Falls State Park, in Coulee City.

**OPPOSITE:** *Biking is an intimate way to view the rolling fields of the Palouse and eastern Washington.*
**THIS PAGE:** *The Dry Falls at sunrise.*

Chapter 6: The Palouse

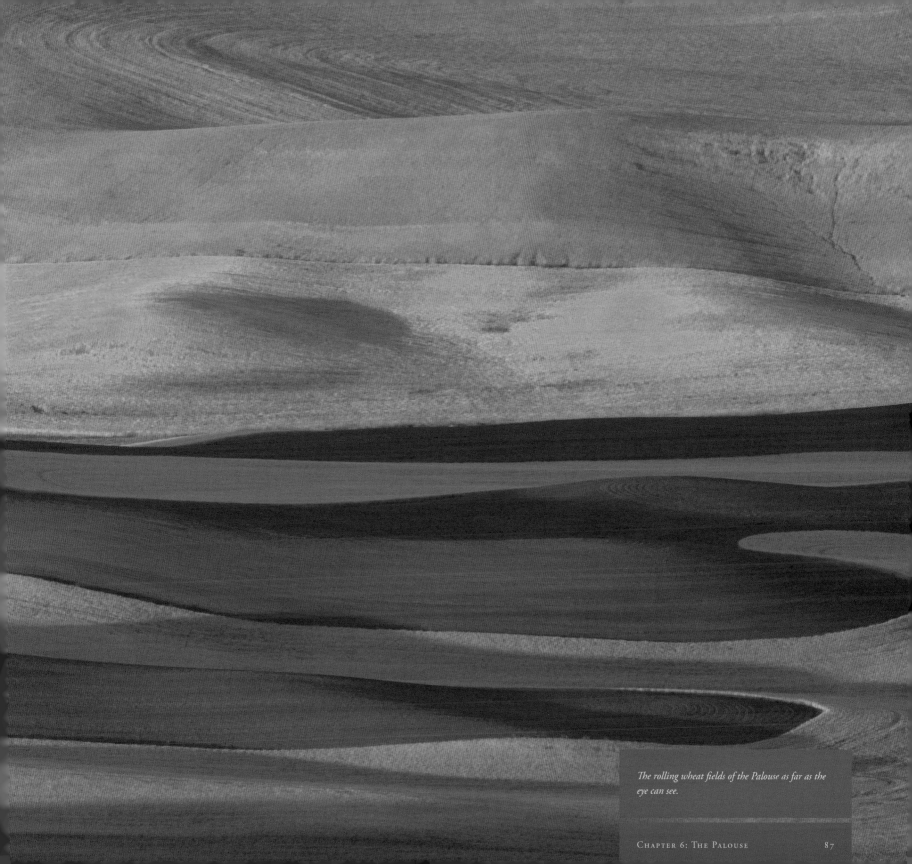

*The rolling wheat fields of the Palouse as far as the eye can see.*

Chapter 6: The Palouse

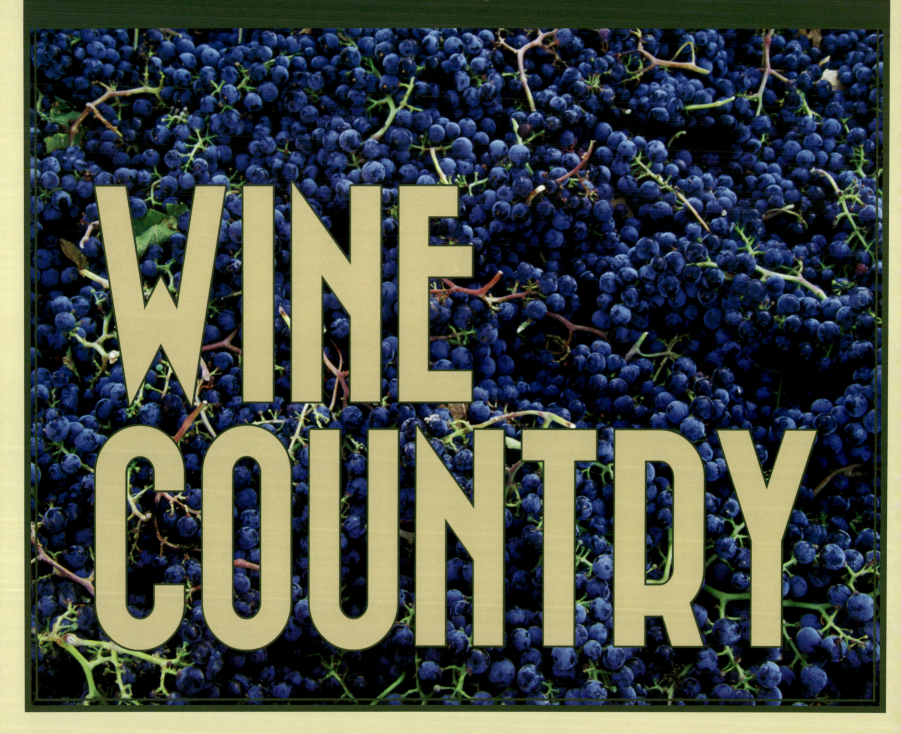

CHAPTER 7

WINE COUNTRY

# GRAPE TRELLISES ADORN THE HILLS

in an endless spectrum of green vines. Syrahs and Cabernets are strung out across one side of the road; concord grapes grow on the other. The valley beckons with fields of grapes and mint, hops, and cherries.

More than 800 wineries now call Washington home. In fact, the state is bested only by California when it comes to the amount of premium wine produced. The grapes in this state have fantastic character due to geographic, climatic, and geological changes over millennia, including glacial floods, volcanic eruptions, and subsequent enormous lava flows that enriched the soil with sand and silt full of basalt, quartz, and mica. Wine country fills the southeastern part of Washington State, where heat rises consistently during long summer days, allowing for ideal ripening conditions, and where it drops precipitously at night, allowing grapes to retain their acidity.

Descend out of the Cascade Mountains alongside the winding Tieton River, and the Yakima Valley unwinds along the east. Yakima itself sits on arid lands only 60 miles southeast of Mount Rainier, surrounded by acres of peach and cherry trees, and fields full of melons and peppers and asparagus. Then come the many vineyards. The Yakima Valley American Viticultural Area (AVA) was the state's first federally recognized AVA and contains a whopping one-third of the state's vineyards. The area is largely encompassed within an even larger AVA—Columbia Valley AVA—and also contains three subregions, Rattlesnake Hills, Snipes Mountain, and the windblown Red Mountain.

Southeast of Yakima, farm towns thrive. There is tiny Toppenish, where Western murals cover downtown buildings, and Grandview, so named for the stunning views of both Mount Rainier and Mount Adams it offers. And there is Prosser, often called the birthplace of Washington wine and home now to both an impressive number of wineries as well as a new wine and culinary center that teaches the history of the industry and wine pairing.

At the far eastern end of the valley, Red Mountain is neither red nor mountainous. Here, in semiarid desert, windblown silt—loess—sits atop Missoula flood glacial deposits, and hot days are dramatically cooled at night by the Yakima River.

*Grape vines cover the hills in Walla Walla wine country.*

**THIS PAGE, CLOCKWISE:** *The process of making wine varies based upon the type of wine, size of the winery, and desires of the winemaker, but all depend on some basic steps: harvesting of the grapes; primary fermentation, during which the grapes are crushed; pressing, when the juice is separated from the skin of the grapes; and secondary fermentation, during which the wine is aged in vessels, such as barrels. Finally, the wine is filtered, bottled, and then enjoyed.* **OPPOSITE:** *One of the first tasting rooms in Walla Walla wine country: Leonetti Cellars.*

The Yakima River flows east to meet the Snake and Columbia Rivers at the Tri-Cities—Richland, Kennewick, and Pasco. For centuries this was a rendezvous point for native tribes such as the Yakima, Cayuse, and Walla Walla from eastern Washington, and the Umatilla from Oregon. The complete 9,000-year-old skeleton of a prehistoric man was found here on the banks of the Columbia River in 1996. Early in modern times, farming was the base of the Tri-Cities economy. All of that changed after 1943 with the founding of the Hanford Site, the world's first full-scale plutonium production reactor. Today, the Tri-Cities are home to a mix of farmers, retirees, engineers, and more.

The wild terrain continues to the east. Some 15 million years ago lava flowed across this part of the state, then cooled into basalt bedrock. Glacial flood waters loaded with quartz and mica created ideal terroir in the central and southern parts of the state. Merlot struts its stuff here in Bordeaux blends, and the heat of the valley makes for rich Syrahs and for dense, lush Cabernets.

THIS PAGE: *Fall colors on display in the Red Mountain vineyards in the Yakima Valley.*
OPPOSITE: *Downtown Walla Walla—in recent years the small college town has become a mecca for oenophiles and wine tourists.*

Brick steeples jut into the downtown Walla Walla skyline. Once a farming town renowned for its peas and sweet onions, Walla Walla has become a college town, thanks to a community college and two private schools—Whitman College and Walla Walla University—as well as a wine-touring destination. The region is packed with vineyards; more than 100 wineries call it home. Move beyond the quaint downtown and it's easy to see what has caused the boom. The stunning landscape turns to rolling hills—great for grape growing—that race southeast toward the foothills of the Blue Mountains, and north toward the historic small towns of Waitsburg and Dayton—home to the state's oldest surviving train station.

Chapter 7: Wine Country

## WALLA WALLA VALLEY WINE COUNTRY

On a south-facing hillside in Walla Walla, Gary Figgins planted his first Cabernet Sauvignon and Riesling grapes in 1974. Soon, an industry was blossoming.

Those first Cabernet grapes would come to be the hallmark varietal of Figgins's Leonetti Cellar. Tasting rooms in Walla Walla are mostly grouped by area. West of town—the vintage loop—are two of the pioneer wineries, both established in the early 1980s. Downtown, a dozen or so wineries line the streets, making for great tasting and strolling, although most of the wineries produce their juice elsewhere in the valley. More than 20 tasting rooms occupy quaint old buildings in the airport area. A handful of wineries cover the hills east of town, while to the south wineries abound on and around J. B. George Road, and all the way to the Oregon border.

OPPOSITE: *A view of vineyards just outside the town of Walla Walla.* THIS PAGE: *On the road to the Blue Mountains. While the majority of the mountain range lies in Oregon, foothills and the Umatilla National Forest area straddle the border between Oregon and Washington.*

CHAPTER 7: WINE COUNTRY

THIS PAGE: *Vineyards for miles.* OPPOSITE: *Wine country isn't only for grapes—apple and cherry orchards also abound.*

THIS PAGE: *Craft beer is also gaining a foothold in wine country. Here, hops dry in a Yakima brewery.*
OPPOSITE: *Hops grow on the bine.*

# HOPPY DAYS

Grapes aren't the only produce with crushing numbers in wine country. Orchards and hops are also plentiful. In fact, Washington grows more apples, pears, and sweet cherries than any other state in the nation. And Washington is a leader in beer, too. Besides the Northwest having brewed a reputation for IPA, it is also a hop-growing haven. A whopping 77+ percent of the nation's hops are grown in the Yakima Valley, and two-thirds of the hops produced in the valley are exported to countries around the world.

America's first post-Prohibition brewpub—the Yakima Brewing & Malting Company, also known as Grant's Brewery Pub—was founded in Yakima in 1982. Now the area is home to breweries, wineries, and the American Hop Museum.

Such high production levels means that Yakima hops can be found in everything from Bud Light to esoteric ales made by Trappist monks, and they can also be found in Yakima Valley beers. The area is home to breweries such as Bale Breaker, Hop Nation, Snipes Mountain, and Yakima Craft Brewing, as well as Swede Hill Distilling and Tieton Cider Works, which both use the local apple bounty.

## UP AND AWAY

Cyclists love Walla Walla perhaps as much as wine enthusiasts love wine. So much so that the local cycling community has created its own bike map. Whether you're up for a blood-pumping ride alongside rolling wheat fields before brunch, or a daylong two-wheel tasting tour on fresh pavement among the wineries south of town on and around J. B. George Road, Walla Walla has it.

Others prefer to float above it all. Thanks to those wonderful thermals that lift out of the desertlike countryside, hot-air balloons conglomerate above wine country every year during the Great Prosser Balloon Rally. Other times during the year, single balloons can be seen hovering over the grapevines and coasting above the valley's rivers.

For golfers in Walla Walla, vineyards and orchards make way for meticulously groomed greens, sand, and high grasses at Wine Valley Golf Club. In Yakima, even the water hazards pay tribute to the valley's fruit: the 17th hole at one resort has an island shaped like an apple.

The region's namesake river is home to rainbow and cutthroat trout. The fishing is so good here that a 75-mile stretch of the Yakima River has been designated as the state's only official Blue Ribbon trout stream.

LEFT: *Hot-air balloons are poised to float above the Leonetti Vineyard. The scene was photographed during the filming of* Wings Over Washington.
THIS PAGE: *Rafting on the Tieton River, as photographed by the film crew for* Wings Over Washington.

CHAPTER 7: WINE COUNTRY

# CHAPTER 8

# COLUMBIA RIVER AND THE GORGE

# FROM THE NORTH, THE MIGHTY COLUMBIA

River rolls more than 1,240 miles, much of it through Washington State. It tumbles out of the Canadian Rockies, then descends across the United States border and into Washington amid pine forests. It slides into the Okanogan River, curls into deepwater kidney-shaped pools, and lazes through high-desert landscapes along the borders of the Colville Indian Reservation. Between the hills surrounding Lake Chelan and into the agricultural hub of Wenatchee, the river winds southward steady and slow. The river gathers into stillness in the 130-mile-long Lake Roosevelt, making a home for sturgeon that can grow longer than eight feet. From there, it spills down 550 feet of concrete when it crosses the Grand Coulee Dam. Then it carves its way south and west through the state, gorging cliffs and pillars out of basalt as it flows.

Around Quincy the Columbia flows into the Ancient Lakes grape-growing region, and scores of green vines grow across cliff tops above the river. Trees of stone and fossil beds of petrified wood—ginkgo trees and Douglas fir, magnolia and witch hazel—as well as Wanapum petroglyphs line the hills west of the river at Vantage. To the east 15 wild horses, cast in steel, gallop across a ridge; this public sculpture, named *Grandfather Cuts Loose the Ponies*, was created as a gift for the state's centennial in 1989. Nearby is the Gorge Amphitheatre, a 20,000-seat concert venue set high atop a basalt bluff overlooking the river.

The Columbia River courses south past orchards and vineyards as it flows into central-eastern Washington by the Hanford Reach National Monument. The US Fish and Wildlife Service's first national monument, near the last nontidal, free-flowing section of the Columbia, is full of remote, hardscrabble lands. The area is marked by extreme heat, sagebrush, tumbleweed, and towering bluffs, and yet nature ekes out an existence here. Mule deer, coyotes, a herd of elk, bald eagles, great blue herons, and sometimes even white pelicans make the monument home. Plutonium reactors—remnants of WWII and the Cold War—also stand on the shore, serving as reminders of the nation's past. As it flows south and into the Tri-Cities—Richland, Kennewick, and Pasco—the Columbia merges with the Yakima and Snake Rivers.

*The White Bluffs edge a free-flowing section of the Columbia River.*

At last, the river turns and begins its more than 309-mile western journey to the Pacific Ocean, creating a natural border for Washington and Oregon. Fruit orchards, vineyards, and wind farms cover otherwise treeless hilltops. The landscape is marked by broad prairies, empty expanses, and towering cliffs. The landscape here can climb from sea level to one-third of a mile above sea level in a matter of moments. Just outside the city of Stevenson columnar basalt cliffs rise 1,000 feet above the water's edge.

As the river cuts a border between Washington and Oregon, it grows wide. Hot desert air meets low-pressure systems from the Cascade Mountains, causing wind to howl. Sometimes during the year the wind can race upriver at more than 35 knots.

The wind brings its own devotees, especially from June through September, when large temperature gradients between the desert climate to the east and the cooler, wetter climate of the Pacific Ocean drive winds. The combination of the winds blowing east and the current flowing west makes for fantastic windsurfing conditions. All summer the waters dazzle with a rainbow of kiteboarders and windsurfers cruising alongside barges.

OPPOSITE: *High on a ridge, fifteen life-size steel statues memorialize the region's long-gone wild horses.*
THIS PAGE: *The sun sets over twenty thousand fans at the Gorge Amphitheater.*

Over a mere 30 miles, between the lands to the east and west of the Cascade Mountains, the climate on the riverbank changes rapidly from arid continental in the east to a wet maritime in the west. Dams line the river, too, and at the westernmost barrier sea lions flock to catch salmon spawning.

Rising out of the river near Vancouver, Washington, is the 848-foot-tall monolith of Beacon Rock, where Lewis and Clark camped during their journey through the Gorge. The water continues on past Portland until finally, with Cape Disappointment on its northern bank, it delivers itself to the Pacific Ocean at Ilwaco, surrounded by rocky headlands and long ribbons of sandy beach.

# LEWIS AND CLARK

On October 10, 1805, Lewis and Clark entered Washington State at the confluence of what are now known as the Clearwater River and the Snake River. On the 16th, they arrived at the confluence of the Snake and the Columbia—at what is now Pasco—becoming the first Euro-Americans to see the Columbia east of the Cascades. The first night they were greeted by a delegation of 200 Wanapum men who arrived in camp singing, beating drums, and chanting a greeting.

Here on the Columbia, salmon replaced buffalo as the primary dietary staple among the native tribes, and, until they passed The Dalles, Lewis and Clark's Corps of Discovery met only Native Americans who had never before encountered white men. Firewood became scarce for the party as they moved from the wooded mountains into southern Washington's treeless, high-desert plains.

At Celilo Falls, the party was faced with difficult portages: the river dropped 38 feet within just a few miles. Only a few miles after they were back in the water, they came to the violent rapids at The Dalles. Finally, on November 2, the party passed through to the broad, flat, and swift waters of the lower Columbia, and fully into the tribal lands of Chinookans, ancestors of today's Yakama, Warm Springs, Umatilla, and Nez Percé nations.

On November 7, the Corps reached a large estuary of the Pacific Ocean, prompting Clark to mistakenly cry "Ocian in view O! the joy." Unfortunately, the party was still 20 miles from the Pacific. Hemmed in by a fierce storm coming off the Pacific, they made camp across from then 70-foot-tall Pillar Rock and waited for a clearing in the weather to begin again. Finally, on November 15—one year, six months, and a day after they had departed St. Louis, Missouri— the Corps reached the Pacific Ocean.

Chapter 8: Columbia River

# DAMS OF THE COLUMBIA

Once wild and unruly, the Columbia River has been much tamed over time. From its headwaters in British Columbia to its exit at the Pacific Ocean, the river basin comprises some 260,000 square miles, and includes 11 dams in Washington State, including the Grand Coulee.

Four US Army Corps of Engineers dams span the river between Oregon and Washington. Farthest east is the 1.4-mile-long McNary Dam, which connects Umatilla County, Oregon, with Benton County, Washington. Below Goldendale, Washington, is the John Day Dam, which features the tallest navigational lock in the States. And 40 miles east of Portland and 145 river miles from the Pacific Ocean, the Bonneville Dam is a destination for many a California sea lion, when salmon and sockeye flock to its fish ladders during spawning season. Upon completion of The Dalles Dam slack water submerged Celilo Falls, an ancient Native American fishing site, cultural hub and one of the oldest continuously inhabited settlement in North America.

**PREVIOUS SPREAD, LEFT:** *The Columbia River provides a natural border between Oregon and Washington State.* **PREVIOUS SPREAD, RIGHT:** *In Charles Marion Russell's* Lewis and Clark on the Lower Columbia River, *Sacagawea guides the two explorers and their crew.* **OPPOSITE:** *Water rushes through the twelve gates of the 1.4-mile-long McNary Dam.* **THIS PAGE:** *A sun-kissed view of the Columbia River Gorge from Beacon Rock.*

CHAPTER 8: COLUMBIA RIVER

## GO FLY A KITE

Outdoor enthusiasts flock to the Columbia River. In the north, the river serves as a destination for recreational boaters and water-skiers, who love to skim the flat waters and duck into hidden coves. In the middle of the state, kayakers, canoers, and jet boaters navigate the last nontidal, free-flowing section of the river at the Hanford Reach National Monument, near the Tri-Cities.

The stretch of river between Oregon and Washington is famed in the adventure sports world. In what is known as the windsurfing capital of the world, kiteboarders and windsurfers cover the Columbia June through September, when winds reliably howl upriver.

The 2012 removal of a dam on the White Salmon River brought white water surging off Mount Adams, to the great delight of rafters who enjoy the river's remarkably consistent flows. The area, with its long and narrow gorges and old-growth Douglas fir groves, is good for hiking, too.

A network of trails branches through Vancouver, Washington, including the paved five-mile Columbia River Renaissance Trail, which features both a beach and views of Mount Hood.

**OPPOSITE:** *A kiteboarder launches at East Point Kite Beach.* **THIS PAGE:** *Windsurfers catch a good west wind.*

CHAPTER 8: COLUMBIA RIVER

THIS PAGE: *The Celilo Falls, a fifteen-thousand-year-old fishing area, in a photo taken a few years before it was flooded by the Dalles Dam.* OPPOSITE: *The Horsethief Butte petroglyphs are a Native American legacy.*

# NATIVE PEOPLE OF THE RIVER

The Columbia River basin has long been a home for Native Americans. The confluence of the Columbia and the Snake Rivers was historically a gathering spot for Sahaptin-speaking people, and it was here that the Wanapum leader, Cutssahnem, presented Lewis and Clark with a charcoal-on-skin map of the river and its tribal nations.

The river was—and still is—a vital fishing area for Native American tribes. When Lewis and Clark entered the Columbia, they discovered Native American fishing villages on the shores every 8 to 10 miles, and the air was constantly scented with the smell of fish smoking and drying. Today, the Yakama Nation maintains active fishing rights on the Columbia.

The Chilluckittequw, Lower Chinook, Clatsop, Willapa, Wahkiakum, and Kathlamet people dominated the areas along the banks of the Columbia for thousands of years.

**OPPOSITE:** *Beacon Rock State Park is a favorite destination for hikers, bikers, and equestrians.*
**THIS PAGE:** *The slithering route of a Snake River tributary.*

Chapter 8: Columbia River

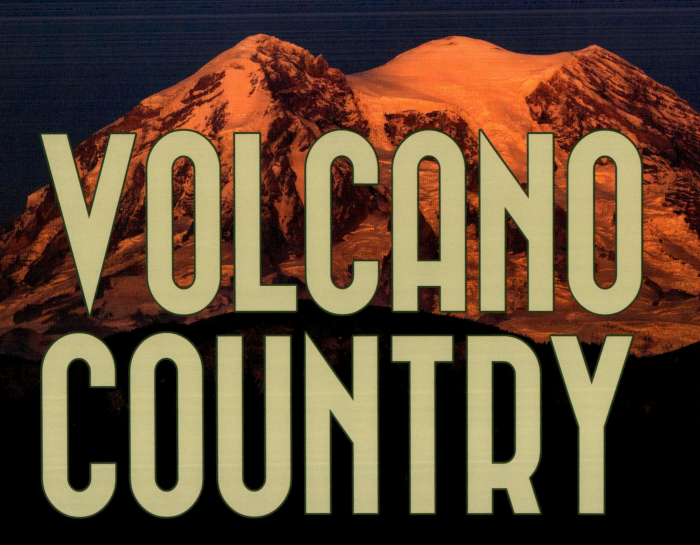

# CHAPTER 9

# VOLCANO COUNTRY

# THE SNOWCAPPED CONE OF VOLCANIC

Mount Rainier soars above the horizon more than 14,000 feet above sea level. In her shadow stand two more volcanoes—Mount Saint Helens, which famously blew her top in 1980, and Mount Adams. To the north, the Cascade Range—which stretches more than 700 miles from Canada to northern California—is largely tectonic uplifts of 400-million-year-old Mesozoic crystalline and metamorphic rocks. In the south, it is volcanic. In fact, Washington State has 10 volcanoes, including Mount Baker and Glacier Peak in the north Cascades. The biggest conglomeration, however, rises in the southwestern section of the state, where Mounts Adams, St. Helens, and Rainier dominate the horizon. These three volcanoes are clustered within 50 miles of each other, providing the region with the nickname Volcano Country.

Tantalizing and icily aloof from afar, up close Mount Rainier captivates. In the northwest corner, near the Carbon River entrance, stands both a rain forest and the lowest-elevation glacier in the Lower 48. On the southeast side, near Ohanapecosh, is an ancient grove of Douglas firs, western red cedars, and hemlocks.

From the valley floor below the mountain, lush green stands of trees wind uphill until they meet high subalpine fields carpeted with wildflowers. Dozens of waterfalls tumble over volcanic rock throughout the mountain's national park. Glaciers creep down mountain peaks to melt into rivers that rage among arboreal giants. Alpine lakes reflect mountaintop and sky upon their surfaces. Mountain climbers clamber over crevasses as they edge their way toward the summit. Elk bugle, eagles soar, and marmots burrow and cavort in the mountain wildness.

A bit above the 5,400-foot level, the Paradise Jackson Visitor Center is surrounded by meadows of mountain wildflowers. Come winter, the fields turn to slopes for sledding, but when the snow is gone the area offers up close views of the Nisqually Glacier.

Small towns cluster around Rainier's flanks. Train cars and the Mount Rainier Scenic Railroad dominate the tiny village of Elbe on Alder Lake. Fishermen flock to Mineral Lake for its stocked trout, while gardeners

*Narada Falls in Mount Rainier National Park.*

head to Mossyrock for its bulb farm and summer blueberry festival. Morton—set on Riffe Lake, nested in the foothills of the Cascade Mountains southwest of Mount Rainier—makes for a nature lover's paradise, while tiny Ashford is a starting point for Mount Rainier climbers planning to summit the mountain. The headquarters for multiple mountain guide outfits and a bunkhouse named for Jim Wittaker, the mountain's more notable denizen (and the first American to reach the summit of Mount Everest), can be found here.

In the shadow of the mighty Tahoma—as the native peoples who lived here called Rainier—stands Mount Saint Helens, notable for its sometimes steaming, concave, horseshoe-shaped crater. Once standing nearly 10,000 feet tall, the mountain was reduced in height by 1,300 feet when it exploded in 1980.

*From left to right are the sister volcanoes of the Cascades: Adams, Ranier, and Saint Helens (Oregon's Mount Hood is in the background).*

Chapter 9: Volcano Country

*Mount Saint Helens erupts on May 18, 1980.*

That explosion sent rock, pumice, and fine particles flowing 13 miles down the North Fork Toutle River, and caused a lateral explosion to tear through the avalanche and create extreme stone-filled winds that flattened nearly 230 miles of forest. Then, for nine hours, ash flew skyward from the volcano and fell across the state and its surroundings.

Today a lava dome rises in the center of the mountaintop's crater. Below it, lakes soft with a floor of ashen sediment ripple, the river has rerouted, and plants and trees have begun to flourish in the once-ash-covered landscape.

Thirty-four miles to the east, Helen's brother mountain, Mount Adams, rises. The mountain's glacier-capped top descends into icefalls on the northern face, and then runs off to form Adams Creek. Trails lace through wildflower meadows and open forests, past glacial streams and traces of lahars and lava flows. To the east is the Yakama Indian Reservation, to the south the massive Columbia River. All over, the mountain is flanked by the dry air of the east, by moisture on the west.

## MOUNT SAINT HELENS, THEN AND NOW

For millions of years, Mount Saint Helens's round cone-like dome stood on the horizon, covered in snow. Then, in 1980, she blew her top. The explosive eruption caved in the mountain's top, creating a horseshoe-shaped crater in its place.

Before the eruption, Spirit Lake lay just north of Mount Saint Helens, surrounded by old-growth forests. Those thick forests prevented much light from seeping to the forest floor and also provided for limited wind. Then came the small earthquakes in mid-March of 1980, hinting that the magma had begun moving.

On May 18, the mountain erupted and the north flank collapsed, producing the largest landslide-debris avalanche in recorded history. The debris scoured the landscape as it raced toward Spirit Lake, and then covered the upper reaches of the North Fork of the Toutle River.

Nearly 230 square miles of forest was either blown down or scorched by debris fields in the eruption. Ash rose in the air and ran in slurries down the mountain. In all, the eruption brought some 500 million tons of ash to Washington, Oregon, Idaho, and Montana, with traces of ash discovered around the world.

Today, Mount Saint Helens is beginning to bloom. Surviving plants rise out of the ash. Forests take hold again. Spirit Lake has been restocked with trout, and Douglas firs root nearby in crevices between volcanic rock.

And still, on occasion, the mountain steams.

**OPPOSITE:** *With beautiful Spirit Lake in the foreground, Mount Saint Helens before the eruption.*
**THIS PAGE:** *Following the eruption, debris covered Spirit Lake, a field of devastation spread more than 17 miles long, and the mountain was reduced in height by more than 1,000 feet.*

OPPOSITE: *Mount Rainier is reflected in a lake within the Mount Rainier National Park.*
THIS PAGE: *There are more than 150 waterfalls within Mount Rainier National Park.*

Chapter 9: Volcano Country

THIS PAGE: *The fifth-tallest mountain in the continental United States, Mount Rainier is climbed by thousands each year.* OPPOSITE, ABOVE: *In this circa 1920s photograph, a climbing group sets out from Paradise in the Mount Rainier National Park.* OPPOSITE, BELOW: *Climbers make camp along the Kautz Glacier Route on Mount Rainier.*

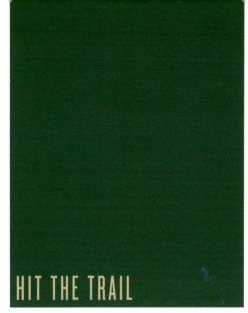

# HIT THE TRAIL

It is virtually impossible not to find a place to hike or explore in the areas around Mounts Rainier, St. Helens, and Adams. There are a number of alpine and backcountry wilderness campsites scattered around Mount Rainier. Four—including Snow Lakes—are an easy hike from the road. There are 27 major glaciers in Mount Rainier National Park, and several are visible from the road or accessible by hiking, including the Emmons Glacier, which can be viewed by hiking a one-mile trail from Mount Rainier's Sunrise Visitor Center.

During summer months, visitors can park at Mount Rainier's Longmire, shuttle to Paradise, and hike the Wonderland Trail back. Come winter, there is snowshoeing and sledding at Paradise. The Mount Tahoma Trail Association maintains 50 miles of backcountry trails—20 miles of which are groomed—just outside Mount Rainier National Park. More adventurous hikers can commit to a 93-mile hike of the entire Wonderland Trail encircling Mount Rainier.

Near Mount Saint Helens, a 2.6-mile round-trip walk delivers the wonder of underground lava-carved caves, known as the Ape Caves. During the summer and fall, hikers can explore the frozen stalactites and stalagmites in the 650-foot-long Guler Ice Cave at Trout Lake, near Mount Adams.

Chapter 9: Volcano Country

**THIS PAGE:** *Mount Adams rises above the clouds.* **OPPOSITE, ABOVE:** *The view of Mount Adams at sunrise.* **OPPOSITE, BELOW:** *A rustic cabin on Mount Adams. Traditional A-frame cabins dot the Cascades.*

WINGS OVER WASHINGTON

# FRESHWATER LAKES PUNCTUATE SEATTLE

and briny Puget Sound edges the city. South of the hilly metropolis, snowcapped Mount Rainier looms. At the northern edge of downtown, the Space Needle rises 605 feet above the Seattle Center, which houses the EMP Museum and Dale Chihuly's dazzling garden of glass while also serving as an eclectic park for city residents. Nearby, seaplanes buzz and sailboats bob at anchor on Lake Union.

Once home to tribes such as the Duwamish, white settlers established themselves in the city in 1851, first at Alki and then in Pioneer Square, which offered access to a deepwater port on Elliott Bay in Puget Sound. Lumber reigned in the beginning, but fishing and shipbuilding soon added to the economy in the late 1880s. By 1889 Seattle was growing by an estimated 1,000 people each month, and 500 new buildings were under construction downtown, most of them made of wood. In June of that year, a devastating fire swept the city, leveling downtown buildings on 116 acres of land.

Seattle has been known to boom and bust; the 1920s depressed lumber and shipbuilding, and the Great Depression worsened things.

Aircraft manufacturer Boeing was founded in the city in 1916, which is how Seattle got one of its many nicknames—the Jet City. Today, the city shines in towers of glass and metal high-rises, and it's known for tech innovation and as a haven for start-ups. At the city's western edge, Pike Place Market's warren of shops and rows of flower stalls bustle as fishmongers and craftspeople call out their wares. West of the market, at the water's edge and atop historic Pier 57, the Seattle Great Wheel spins colorfully on its axis. To the south—past Pier 54, Ivar's Acres of Clams, and Ye Olde Curiosity Shop, in a building built by the Northern Pacific Railway, and beyond the Washington State Ferry terminal—stand CenturyLink Field (home of the NFL Seahawks and the Seattle Sounders football club) and the Mariners' Safeco Field.

Eclectic neighborhoods span out in all directions from downtown Seattle. Amazon's headquarters fills the streets of South Lake Union, while just to the northwest, Queen Anne Hill beckons for spectacular views of downtown and the Sound.

*The Great Wheel is reflected in the waters of Elliott Bay.*

Chapter 10: Seattle

ABOVE: *A view of Seattle's waterfront with the skyline behind it.* BELOW: *The Port of Seattle is the fourteenth-largest in the United States.* OPPOSITE: *The southwest view of Elliott Bay and the Port of Seattle from Seattle's Space Needle.*

On the north end of freshwater Lake Union is Gas Works Park. The site of a former coal gasification plant, which operated from 1906 to 1956, it is now a 20-acre public park. The Lake Washington Ship Canal runs through Lake Union connecting the saltwater Puget Sound to the 22-mile-long freshwater Lake Washington to the east.

The former Scandinavian enclave and fishing neighborhood of Ballard rests along the canal and near the shores of Puget Sound, full now of restaurants, shops, and pubs along brick-paved streets. Funky Fremont, with its statue of Lenin and public troll sculpture below the Aurora Bridge, lies between Ballard and Gas Works Park. To the north are the hamlets of Wallingford and Green Lake, with an eponymous lake and 259-acre park at its center.

To the northeast—east of Lake Union and lingering on the banks of Lake Washington and the Montlake Cut (which connects Lakes Washington and Union)—is the 703-acre University of Washington.

Chapter 10: Seattle

Hills climb east out of downtown up to where Capitol Hill—long the hub of Seattle's LGBT community—stands decked out in restaurants and clubs, flush with hipsters and students. South from here is the Central District, historically among the city's most racially and ethnically diverse neighborhoods. On the shores of Lake Washington is Leschi, a former campsite of the Nisqually Tribe's Chief Leschi, and today home to condominiums and bungalows, American Craftsman- and Tudor-style homes, and mid-century ramblers. Farther south is the Mount Baker neighborhood—bounded on the east by Lake Washington and offering up views of the namesake peak in the distance—and the Rainier Valley, one of the most culturally and economically diverse communities in the entire Pacific Northwest.

Southwest of downtown, Alki Beach in West Seattle juts into Puget Sound, granting views of downtown dappled in lights, of ferries cruising, and of kiteboarders surfing the sound. Every summer pirates make landfall on this spit of land as part of Seafair—a monthlong, citywide celebration that includes parades and hydroplane races, jet plane performances, and torchlight runs.

Wings Over Washington

*The Seattle skyline as seen from Lake Union. Mount Rainier lies in the distance.*

Chapter 10: Seattle

THIS PAGE: *The city of Bellevue lies on the opposite side of Lake Washington from Seattle. Two floating bridges connect Seattle with the Eastside.* OPPOSITE: *The 268-foot Snoqualmie Falls is about a half hour east of Seattle. It was photographed during the filming of* Wings Over Washington. NEXT PAGE, ABOVE: *A fruit and vegetable stand at the Pike Place Market, one of hundreds of vendor stands in the century-old public market.* NEXT PAGE, BELOW: *Three Seattle icons converge: the Monorail, the Space Needle, and the Experience Music Project.*

East of the city, technology booms. Bellevue rises in skyscrapers on the eastern shore of Lake Washington. Early settlers logged the land, a community of family farms took root in the early 1900s, and in 1979 Microsoft arrived in the city to create a tech center here. Today, Microsoft makes its headquarters east of the city, in Redmond, and start-ups and spin-offs proliferate alongside companies like T-Mobile and Expedia.

Everywhere beyond the Emerald City, mountains surround. The Olympic Mountains fill the western horizon line past Puget Sound, Mount Baker thrusts itself into the sky to the north, and beyond Bellevue the land climbs into the foothills of the Cascade Range. In Fall City, to the east, Snoqualmie Falls crashes 270 feet to the river below—100 feet higher than Niagara Falls. Fall City gives way to the green of pines, the brown of boughs, and to slate-colored stone as the Cascade Mountains rise up to create the divide that keeps western Washington moist and verdant and eastern Washington lush with orchards and grapevines.

# LANDMARKS OF SEATTLE

Choosing just one iconic experience in Seattle is almost impossible. North of downtown is the Seattle Center, home of the Space Needle, built for the 1962 World's Fair, and the Experience Music Project museum. In the heart of downtown is the Columbia Center, which soars 902 feet above the streets and has the highest public viewing area—the 73rd-floor Sky View Observatory—west of the Mississippi. Blocks away in historic Pioneer Square is Seattle's original skyscraper, Smith Tower, which opened in 1914. Cruise ships line the waterfront south of the Olympic Sculpture Park. Once an industrial site, the nine-acre plot between train tracks and Elliott Bay is now home to roughly 20 outdoor sculptures. South of the park along the waterfront are the Seattle Aquarium, historic piers teeming with life, and Pier 57, home to Seattle's own Great Wheel.

Probably the best-recognized and most visited spot in Seattle is the Pike Place Market. Located on a steep hill, and overlooking Elliott Bay, the market is among the busiest farmers' markets in the nation. About 240 independent businesses weave throughout: the lower level arcades are full of novelty stores, arts and crafts shops, and restaurants; and the main level is home to fishmongers, florists, produce vendors, and small creameries. A healthy busker community makes the market's cobbled streets a performance space, including along the sidewalk outside the original Starbucks. Established in 1907, Pike Place Market is more than a tourist destination. It is the bustling center of Seattle's farm-fresh, locally sourced, artisanal and specialty foods. The market is home to people, too. The windows and balconies above hint at the apartment homes of the approximately 400 people—most of whom are low-income seniors—who dwell there.

# GET OUTSIDE!

While Seattle may best be known for its coffee, tech, and music, it is also one of the most outdoor-focused regions of the country. Just one glance at the ski and bicycle racks attached to every other car gives you a clear idea of what many Seattleites do on their weekends.

Fortunately, they have a wealth of options—summer or winter. When temperatures drop and winter rain descends on the city, you can be sure the snow is dumping elsewhere, drawing downhill and cross-country skiers, snowboarders, and snowshoers to the two mountain ranges near Seattle: the Olympics and the Cascades. Closest to Seattle is Snoqualmie Pass, less than an hour's drive away.

On clearer days, Seattleites jump on their bicycles or put on their running shoes to make use of the Burke-Gilman Trail, a 19-mile recreational trail that passes through Seattle, or head to one of the many parks, including Discovery Park, a 534-acre park on the shores of Puget Sound, and Seward Park, a 300-acre park on a Lake Washington peninsula.

With plenty of water in and around the city, many look to it for recreation. If the sun is out—and even if it isn't—you will find sailors, rowers, paddleboarders, and kayakers plying the waters of Lake Union, Elliott Bay, and Lake Washington.

Chapter 10: Seattle

# UNIVERSITY OF WASHINGTON

Spread out on 703 acres of land, above a cut that connects Seattle's Lake Union to Lake Washington, is the University of Washington. Home to a quad that turns pink and white with cherry blossoms every spring, the research university is among the oldest universities on the West Coast.

The school was established on 10 acres downtown in 1861, and opened officially in November of that year—28 years before Washington State joined the Union. The UW moved to its present location in 1895. It now has three campuses that offer over 531 degree options across 294 programs and educates more than 55,000 students every year. The School of Medicine is among the top in the nation, and since 1974 the UW has been the largest recipient of federal research funding among all public universities in the nation, and second among all public and private universities in the country.

Referred to informally as U-Dub, the university sits on the shores of Lake Washington's Union Bay and Lake Union's Portage Bay. At the southeastern edge of campus is U-shaped Husky Stadium, with its open eastern end that overlooks Lake Washington, the Cascade Mountains, and, on a clear day, Mount Rainier.

PREVIOUS PAGE: *A skier takes on the Slot Couloir at Mount Snoqualmie. This climb-in peak is popular among extreme skiers—nearby are Snoqualmie Pass mainstays Alpental and Snoqualmie.* OPPOSITE: *Each spring the cherry blossoms bloom in the Quad at University of Washington.* THIS PAGE: *Fans fill Husky Stadium, while maritime tailgaters watch from the water of Lake Washington.*

CHAPTER 10: SEATTLE

THIS PAGE: *Seafair is one of Seattle's most enduring traditions, and the hydroplane races on Lake Washington are a highlight.* OPPOSITE, ABOVE: *US Navy Blue Angels soar during the Seafair air show.* OPPOSITE, BELOW: *A vintage hydroplane,* Miss Budweiser, *zooms past.*

## SEATTLE BOOM

Like any town with a history of booms and busts, it was industry that precipitated much of Seattle's growth, and in the late 1800s and early 1900s, dominated—particularly after Weyerhaeuser purchased 900,000 acres of timberland and began shipping its harvest east.

But one timber baron wasn't satisfied with just selling trees. William Boeing's vision of flight gave birth to the Boeing Company in 1916. Over the course of two world wars and a global change in business, Boeing became—and remains—one of the biggest companies in the world.

By the 1980s, another company emerged to dominate the Northwest horizon: Microsoft. Although located across the waters of Lake Washington in Redmond, the technology giant became one of the region's largest employers—and a harbinger of the tech industry to come.

In the 2000s, e-commerce giant Amazon fostered another boom. And sixteen years later, Amazon's growth continues to change the landscape of the city.

While cutting-edge industries have dominated Seattle's economy, they are not the only companies contributing to the Seattle vibe. The jet city is also known for its coffee, music, and niceness. Starbucks, Sub Pop, and Nordstrom—a company founded by a miner with his Klondike gold rush haul—help to define the world's impression of Seattle.

**OPPOSITE, ABOVE:** *Known as the Red Barn, Boeing's original manufacturing plant is an icon of the company.* **OPPOSITE, BELOW:** *The original Starbucks is located in the Pike Place Market.* **THIS PAGE:** *Nordstrom's flagship store is located in downtown Seattle, not far from John Nordstrom's original shoe store.*

THIS PAGE: *The* Wings Over Washington *crew and Griffith family on location.* OPPOSITE: *Construction is underway on the pier.*

# THE MAKING OF WINGS OVER WASHINGTON

WINGS OVER WASHINGTON BEGAN WITH A VISION INSPIRED BY THE GRIFFITH FAMILY'S love of Seattle and Washington State. They wanted a way to share that passion with every person who visits Miners Landing—and they wanted it to be thrilling, memorable, and true to their own Washington experiences. A simulated flight over the entire state seemed like the perfect way to do this.

To create Wings Over Washington, the Griffiths went to experts who had worked on similar attractions. It took a huge creative and technical team to design an experience that begins the moment guests walk onto Miners Landing and continues until they leave.

Super 78, a company based in Los Angeles, led the creative development and worked with every vendor—graphic designers, sign makers, totem pole carvers, lighting designers, music composers, a ride-system manufacturer, architects, construction teams, animatronics fabricators, and costume designers—to create the full Wings Over Washington experience.

Every step was meticulously planned. The Griffiths came up with a wish list of locations to be featured in the film—places they knew captured the essence of Washington State. In the end, Wings Over Washington provides guests stunning views of 14 iconic Washington sites.

Unlike in a traditional movie theater where the screen is flat, the screen for Wings Over Washington is curved. This allows theatergoers to have an immersive experience—they feel as if they are flying, like the eagle in the film, over the entire state. To maximize the feeling of flying, the film was shot with a custom spherical lense and in 5K high-definition digital video. And to ensure the image is crisp, the film is projected through state-of-the-art laser illumination projectors.

But they didn't stop there. To pull viewers in to the film, the team added action whenever they could: hot-air balloons in Walla Walla, river rafters on the Tieton River, hydroplanes and the US Navy Blue Angels at Seattle's Seafair. Altogether, the experience is heart pounding, dizzying, and unforgettable.

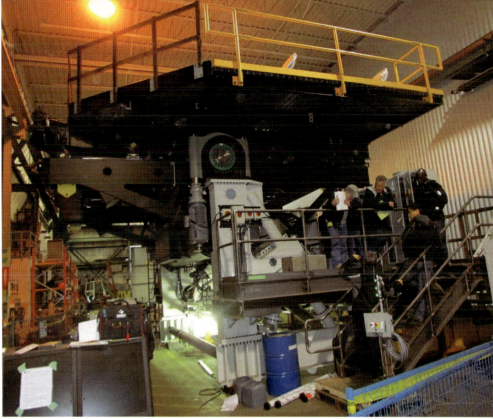
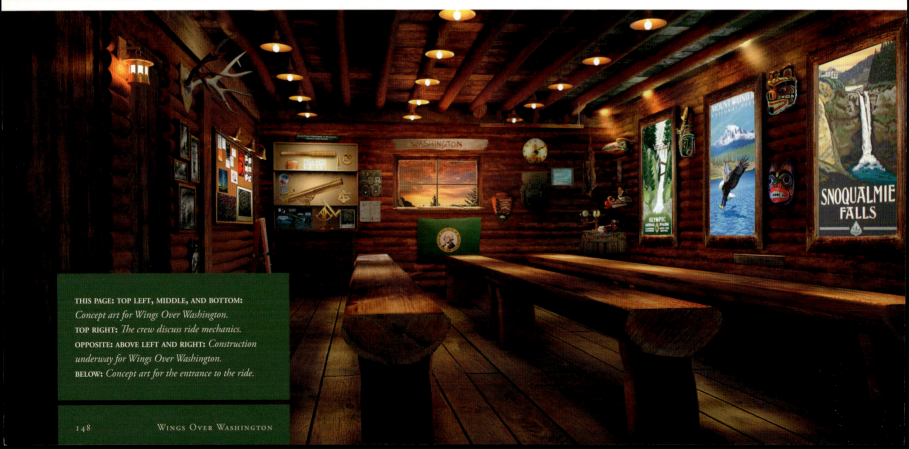

THIS PAGE: TOP LEFT, MIDDLE, AND BOTTOM:
*Concept art for Wings Over Washington.*
TOP RIGHT: *The crew discuss ride mechanics.*
OPPOSITE: ABOVE LEFT AND RIGHT: *Construction underway for Wings Over Washington.*
BELOW: *Concept art for the entrance to the ride.*

# ACKNOWLEDGMENTS

Thank you so much to the many people who worked tirelessly to make the Wings Over Washington attraction and book a reality; your hard work, dedication, and creativity are an inspiration. Special thanks to writer Julie H. Case.

# ABOUT MINERS LANDING

Miners Landing, located on Pier 57 on Seattle's historic waterfront, is more than just a pier. On August 17, 1896, the SS *Portland* docked near the site of what is now the pier. On board was a ton of gold, brought back from the Yukon by 68 lucky prospectors. The landing of the *Portland* made headlines across the world, triggering the Klondike gold rush and turning Seattle into a boomtown.

Over the next century, Pier 57 was a shipping terminal and then used for fish processing before being acquired by the Port of Seattle. In the 1980s, the pier was purchased by the Griffith family, who owns it to this day.

Since then, Pier 57 has become the site of multiple beloved Seattle attractions, including restaurants the Crab Pot and the Fisherman's Restaurant, as well as the Great Wheel. Wings Over Washington is its most recent addition. The pier continues to be owned and operated by the Griffiths.

# IMAGE CREDITS

Cover

© Aurora Photos/Alamy.

Design elements used throughout

© FloridaStock/Shutterstock; © Zack Frank/Shutterstock.

Map

p. iv: Created by Anna Curtis; © tomograf/iStockphoto; © pop_jop/iStockphoto.

Introduction

p. 2: © Miners Landing. p. 3: Courtesy Griffith Family.

Chapter 1: Coastline

p. 4: © Brian Harrison/Tacoma News Tribune/MCT via Getty Images. p. 5: © Josh Trefethen; © Mint Images/Getty Images. p. 6–7: © Peter Horree/Alamy. p. 7: © age fotostock/Alamy; © Pixtal/Super Stock. p. 8: © Dennis Frates/Alamy. p. 9: © Howard Snyder/Aurora/Getty Images. p. 10: © Aurora Photos/Alamy. p. 11: Courtesy Kari Neumeyer, Northwest Indian Fisheries Commission; © Duane Burelson/Alamy; Courtesy Lydia Miller-Parker-Vogel/Makah Cultural & Resource Center. p. 12: © Miners Landing Press. p. 13: Courtesy Cherie Christensen, Saltwater People Historical Society; © University of Washington Libraries, Special Collections, NA 1340. p. 14: © Rhys Logan Photography. p. 15: © Paul Edmonson/Mint Images/Getty Images. p. 16: Courtesy Library of Congress. p. 17: Courtesy Charles Deering McCormick Library of Special Collections, Northwestern University Libraries; © Art by Jim Hart, photographed by Jessica Bushey/Museum of Anthropology, University of British Columbia.

Chapter 2: Olympic Peninsula

p. 18: © Wolfgang Kaehler/LightRocket/Getty Images. p. 19: Universal Images Group/Getty Images. p. 20: © Jon Bilious/Alamy. p. 21: © Design Pics Inc/Alamy. p. 22: © Bill Hinton Photography/Moment Open/Getty Images. p. 23: © James Randklev/DigitalVision/Getty Images. p. 24: © MacDuff Everton/National Geographic Creative; © Michael Hanson/National Geographic Creative. p. 24–25: © The Washington Post/Getty Images. p. 26: Gemma/Moment Open/Getty Images. p. 27: © Rick Pisio/RWP Photography/Alamy. p. 28–29: © Purestock/Alamy. p. 29: © Danita Delimont/Alamy; Courtesy United States Navy. p. 30–31: © Miners Landing Press. p. 31: © Miners Landing Press.

Chapter 3: Puget Sound

p. 32: Courtesy Ingrid Taylar Photography. p. 33: © Jim Lundgren/Alamy. p. 34: © Radius/Super Stock. p. 35: © Edmund Lowe/Alamy; © Greg Reed Photography. p. 36–37: © Kevin Ebi/Alamy. p. 37: © Liz O. Baylen/Los Angeles Times/Getty; © Bill

Gozansky/Alamy. p. 38–39: © Crystal Craig/Dreamstime. p. 40: © Jon Cornforth/Cornforth Photography; © BlueGreen Pictures/Super Stock. p. 40–41: © Dinodia Photos/Alamy. p. 42–43: © Courtesy University of Washington Libraries, Special Collections, UW 5366. p. 44: Courtesy Rhonda Porter. p. 45: © Brad Mitchell/Alamy; © John Terence Turner/Alamy.

### Chapter 4: San Juan Islands

p. 46: © Terry Donnelly/Alamy. p. 47: © Edmund Lowe/Flickr Flash/Getty Images. p. 48: © Richard Wong/Alamy; © Danita Delimont/Alamy; © Edmund Lowe/Alamy. p. 49: © Edmund Lowe/Alamy. p. 50: Chris Cheadle/Alamy. p. 51: © Danita Delimont/Alamy. p. 52–53: © Itsik Marom/Alamy. p. 54: © Glasshouse Images/Alamy. p. 55: Courtesy Tari Gunstone. p. 56–57: Courtesy Anacortes Kayaking Tours. p. 57: © Marjorie McBride/Alamy; © Itsik Marom/Alamy. p. 58: © Itsik Marom/Alamy. p. 59: © Miners Landing Press.

### Chapter 5: North Cascades

p. 60: © Jordan Siemens/DigitalVision/Getty Images. p. 61: © Mark Newman/Lonely Planet Images/Getty Images; © Inge Johnsson/Alamy. p. 62: © Danita Delimont/Gallo Images/Getty Images. p. 63: © Terry Donnelly/Alamy. p. 64: © PBstock/Alamy. p. 65: Dave Blackey/All Canada Photos/Getty Images. p. 66–67: © John Elk III/Alamy. p. 68: © Cliff Leight/Aurora/Getty Images. p. 69: © Spring Images/Alamy. p. 70: © Inge Johnsson/Alamy. p. 70–71: © age fotostock/Getty Images. p. 72: © Image Source/Alamy. p. 73: © Brett Baunton/Alamy.

### Chapter 6: The Palouse and Eastern Washington

p. 74: © Gary Weathers/Tetra Images/Getty Images. p. 75: © Dennis Frates/Alamy. p. 76: © JRJ-Photo/Getty Images. p. 77: © Dennis Frates/Alamy. p. 78: © Northwest Museum of Arts & Culture. p. 78–79: © Don Geyer/Alamy. p. 80–81: © John Barger/Alamy. p. 81: Courtesy Colville National Forest Service; © Danita Delimont/Gallo Images/Getty Images. p. 82: © William Mancebo/Getty Images Sport/Getty Images; © Greg Davis/Alamy. p. 83: © Danita Delimont/Alamy. p. 84: © Dave Schiefelbein/Photographer's Choice/Getty Images. p. 85: © Danita Delimont/Alamy. p. 86–87: © Julie Quarry/Alamy.

### Chapter 7: Wine Country

p. 88: © Greg Vaughn/Alamy. p. 89: © Danita Delimont/Alamy. p. 90: © Zach Holmes/Alamy; Patrick Bennett/Super Stock; © Danita Delimont/Gallo Images/Getty Images. p. 91: Courtesy Figgins Family/Leonetti Cellars. p. 92: © Danita Delimont/Alamy. p. 93: © Danita Delimont/Alamy. p. 94–95: © Andrea Johnson Photography. p. 95: © Danita Delimont/Alamy. p. 96: © Danita Delimont/Alamy. p. 97: © Design Pics Inc/Alamy. p. 98: Courtesy Mat Trogner/Allagash Brewery. p. 99: © Design Pics Inc/Alamy. p. 100–101: © Miners Landing Press. p. 101: © Miners Landing Press.

### Chapter 8: Columbia River and the Gorge

p. 102: © Mike DeCesare/age fotostock/Super Stock. p. 103: © Lee Rentz Photography. p. 104: © Chris Boswell/Alamy. p. 105: Courtesy Matthew Lamb/Live Nation. p. 106: Dave Schiefelbein/The Image Bank/Getty Images. p. 107: © Private Collection/Bridgeman Images. p. 108: © Earl Roberge/Science Source/Getty Images. p. 109: Courtesy Don Pyle. p. 110: © Richard Hallman/Aurora/Getty Images. p. 111: © George Osterag/Alamy. p. 112: © Marquette University Archives. p. 113: © Matthew Heinrichs/Alamy. p. 114: © Greg Vaughn/Alamy. p. 115: © Kevin Schafer/Alamy.

### Chapter 9: The Volcanoes

p. 116: © Kevin Ebi/Alamy. p. 117: © Greg Vaughn/Alamy. p. 118–119: © Joel Guay/Shodanphotos/Moment Open/Getty Images. p. 120–121: © Flirt/Alamy. p. 122: © Harald Sund/Photographer's Choice/Getty Images. p. 123: Courtesy Peter Lipman/USGS Cascades Volcano Observatory. p. 124: © Mint Images Limited/Alamy. p. 125: © Greg Vaughn/Alamy. p. 126: © Corey Rich/Aurora/Getty Images. p. 127: © NPS/Alamy; © Brent Winebrenner/Lonely Planet Images/Getty Images. p. 128–129: © Sunset Avenue Productions/Photodisc/Getty Images. p. 129: © Kevin Wells/Alamy; © Darlisa Black Photography.

### Chapter 10: Seattle

p. 130: © Miners Landing Press. p. 131: © Simon Crumpton/Alamy. p. 132: © Charles Donaldson/EyeEm/Getty Images; © Edmund Lowe Photography/Shutterstock. p. 133: © Ron Buskirk/Alamy. p. 134–135: © Panoramic Images/Getty Images. p. 136: © John & Lisa Merrill/Photodisc/Getty Images. p. 137: © Miners Landing Press. p. 138: © Radek Hofman/Alamy; © Curved Light USA/Alamy. p. 139: © Mint Images/Getty Images. p. 140: © Greg Vaughn/Alamy. p. 141: © Scott Eklund/Red Box Picutres. p. 142: © Miners Landing Press. p. 143: © William Perry/Dreamstime; © MOHAI, Seattle Post-Intelligencer Collection. p. 144: © Museum of History & Industry, Seattle; © Chuck Pefley/Alamy. p. 145: Courtesy Jason Butts Photography.

### Making of the Film

p. 146–149: All images © Miners Landing Press.

### Backmatter

p. 158: © Danita Delimont/Alamy.